THE BEAST
of
EXMOOR

by the same author

CAT COUNTRY

THE BEAST
of
EXMOOR

AND OTHER MYSTERY PREDATORS
OF BRITAIN

Di Francis

JONATHAN CAPE
LONDON

First published 1993
© Di Francis 1993
Jonathan Cape, 20 Vauxhall Bridge Road, London SW1V 2SA

Di Francis has asserted her right under the Copyright, Designs and
Patents Act, 1988 to be identified as the author of this work

A CIP catalogue record for this book is available from the British
Library

ISBN 0–224–03725–0 hardback
0–224–03665–3 paperback

Phototypeset by Deltatype Ltd, Ellesmere Port
Printed in Great Britain by Mackays of Chatham PLC, Chatham, Kent

Contents

Illustrations

Dedicated to Professor Charles Thomas and Dr Bernard Heuvelmans for their advice and encouragement and to Andy and Jan Buchanan, Anne and Dil Maggs and Lynn and Steve Fairclough, for their help and friendship.

And to all the farmers, gamekeepers, police officers, marines, and other witnesses who have come forward to tell of their sightings of mystery big cats.

Not forgetting my editor, Tony Colwell for his support and help during the final preparation of the book.

Thank you all.

You must not say that this cannot be, or that that is contrary to nature. You do not know what Nature is, or what she can do; and nobody knows, not even Sir Roderick Murchison, or Professor Owen, or Professor Sedgwick, or Professor Huxley, or Mr Darwin, or Professor Faraday, or Mr Grove ... They are very wise men; and you must listen respectfully to all they say: but even if they should say, which I am sure they never would, 'That cannot exist. That is contrary to nature,' you must wait a little and see; for perhaps even they may be wrong.

The Water-Babies, Charles Kingsley

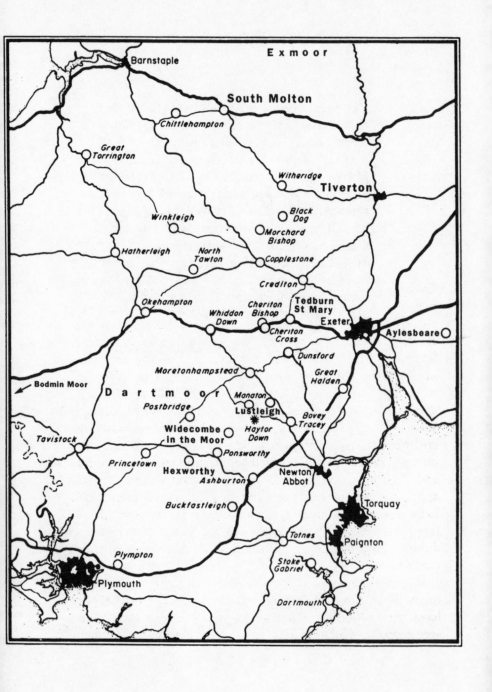

Beginnings

On or about 20–21st June 1991 a Labrador-size cat was seen near the village of Watchet in Somerset, close to Exmoor. According to Dr Gerald Legg, Keeper of Biology at the Booth Museum in Brighton, who reported the sighting in a letter to the *Mammal Society News No. 87*, the two independent witnesses were 'not the type of people who would be mistaken in what they saw'. The animal was approximately 34 inches long with bands of white, orange and silver round its body. It seems the witnesses saw the creature sitting on a mound while they were travelling north on a private railway. They watched it jump from the mound and disappear quickly into the countryside. 'The general appearance, shape and manner of the creature was feline,' Dr Legg wrote. 'I know there are all sorts of strange records of large cats seen in Britain,' he went on, 'many of extremely dubious nature. However I feel that this case merits further examination.'

It is not as isolated a case of a reliable sighting as Dr Legg might think. For the best part of the twentieth century people have been reporting unknown large felines that they have seen roaming wild in Britain. Eight years before the Watchet sighting the biggest cat-hunt ever mounted in this country was taking place nearby in search of the 'Beast of Exmoor'. At that time the world of science preferred to ignore the substantial anecdotal evidence of large killer cats on the prowl, with the sort of dismissive remark as to its efficacy that even today Dr Legg, who wishes to be taken seriously, could not bring himself to leave out of his report. But things have changed. No longer can the Ministry of Agriculture, the police, Britain's farmers and hundreds, if not thousands of witnesses be left in limbo by a scientific fraternity that makes up its mind about the existence or otherwise of unrecognised predators at large before undertaking any serious research into the matter.

The first but, as I will argue, not the overriding explanation for the presence of exotic cats wild in the British countryside is that they have escaped or been released from private ownership, or from zoos or circuses. To provide adequate housing for big cats and pay the feed bills, zoos and wildlife parks have to attract a large number of paying visitors. The economic problems were revealed only too dramatically in 1992 when the Zoological Society of London announced that London Zoo faced closure due to increased running costs and the falling number of visitors.

The 1976 Dangerous Wild Animals Act attempted to halt the indiscriminate owning of exotic or wild animals. It was aimed at poorly kept collections, and at preventing individuals from keeping unusual pets such as big cats in insecure environments, like their own back yards. An inspection and licence system was set up to control the owning of all wild animals, including the potentially dangerous species.

Even if the Act is successful in the long term, some say it has made the immediate problem worse. Owners faced with fines when the new regulations came into force swiftly dumped their exotic pets around the countryside, leaving sometimes dangerous animals, such as leopards, to fend for themselves.

In the past the escape or release of species other than cats has had a marked effect upon the fauna of Britain. The native red and roe deer now compete for grazing with the muntjac, the sika and the fallow deer that once were confined to private estates. The red squirrel now retains a very small area of its natural habitat, having been replaced by the American grey which has established itself in the wild since it was brought over from the New World. Commercially imported mink have escaped from fur farms in sufficient numbers to cause serious problems in some areas for the native bird population. Less damaging are the small herds of wallabies that have established themselves in various locations in Britain, unlike the coypu and porcupines which have bred so successfully that they are now officially classed by the Ministry of Agriculture as pests.

Colonisation by foreign species is not a recent problem. Rabbits are believed to have been brought to Britain, by the Normans, as fur and meat animals and certainly outlived their welcome centuries ago. The common brown rat used traders' ships to aid its distribution around the world, replacing the black rat that had arrived in Britain by similar means from South-east Asia centuries earlier.

With such a long list of thriving imports, the suggestion that there are successful feral exotic cats in Britain should cause no surprise. There are plenty of remote places remaining in Britain to accommodate them and an abundant food supply of both wild and domestic prey animals.

My investigation into the possibility of big cats living wild in the countryside began when I wrote an article for a West Country magazine about reports of a strange puma-size black cat in the area of Tedburn St Mary in Devon. Some witnesses even claimed to have seen a cub running with the adult. While making a search around the heavily forested area, I found tracks that seemed to support the witnesses's claims, and suddenly my own personal odyssey had begun.

To begin with I knew very little about the big cat species of the modern world but as I became more involved I studied the cat family, both past and present, and what I discovered gave me cause for concern. The animal seen at Tedburn St Mary had been black, and as there has never been a captive black puma on record, then it was highly unlikely that it was a puma. A more likely candidate for the title of Tedburn Cat was the leopard as this species frequently produces a melanistic or black form, commonly known as the black panther. If witnesses were not lying, or mistaken, then Mid-Devon appeared to be harbouring a feral leopard which had been reported over a period of at least eleven years. If a cub had been seen, there had to be a pair of adults! A pair of breeding leopards at large in the British countryside was a terrifying thought. To a leopard, man could represent part of the food chain, as primates are included in its natural diet.

Accepting the possibility that the Tedburn cat was a breeding female, I began to search for a male by studying reports of sightings of big cats in other parts of Devon. To my surprise, I unearthed hundreds of witnesses claiming to have seen leopard-size cats over many years, some reports going back to the 1930s. A number of these spoke of large black panthers.

Living at the time in South Devon, I started virtually on my own doorstep, which was dominated by the sprawling Dartmoor National Park. Over these 365 square miles of moorland and granite hills are scattered numerous hill farms and dense forestry plantations. To the north lies the second famous National Park, the rolling bracken-covered hills of Exmoor which flow across into the neighbouring county of Somerset. Both rather barren landscapes are surrounded by the valleys and lower slopes of rich agricultural land. Cattle graze the lusher lowlands while the high tors and bleak moors are in the main given over to hardy hill sheep.

That in 1979 the hill farms were facing huge stock losses was revealed in an article published in the *Mid-Devon Advertiser*:

the Tedburn pub in a very distressed state, the woman overcome with shock. They said they had been driving along the main Exeter to Okehampton road when an enormous black cat had leapt out in front of them so suddenly that they had been unable to avoid hitting it. The continuous stream of traffic had prevented them stopping but they had felt bound to report the incident as they were afraid they had killed someone's pet.

The couple calmed down and continued their journey. Afterwards the incident was passed off as the holidaymakers having hit a large domestic cat, and forgotten. Three weeks later, Tedburn teenager Mark Bastin was rabbiting with his dog along the road verge when he discovered the carcase of a black animal the size of a Labrador dog. It was badly decomposing and difficult to identify, but he returned home to tell his father he had found the body of a dog that had been killed by having its face smashed.

'It was horrible,' he said, 'someone must have smashed in its head with a shovel. There was no injury or blood, but the face was actually flat, as if the nose had been pushed in.'

The body was discovered in the area where the couple had claimed to have hit the huge black cat. Unfortunately the two stories were not linked until eighteen months later, by which time, despite a search of the verge, nothing remained of the mystery carcase. If it had been the body of a cat the size of a Labrador dog, that would be enough to explain the flattened face and the lack of apparent facial injury. The boy could not have expected to be looking at the short muzzle of a feline rather than the long jaw of a dog.

But it was not only Devon that appeared to play host to unknown large felines. My own search soon crossed borders, counties and even countries. From Cornwall to Caithness eyewitnesses were claiming to have encountered large mystery cats, farm stock was falling prey to unknown predators and the authorities were ignoring the situation. With no bodies available for examination, sightings were

Dartmoor farmers who accept that they might lose 10 per cent of the sheep they run on the moor annually are becoming alarmed at their increasing losses, which many are reluctant to put down to natural wastage.

Mr Dick Perryman of Manaton has lost fifty ewes and lambs over the past year. He has advertised the loss in case some have strayed into other flocks but so far has had none returned and is not optimistic about getting them back.

Mr Harold Wonnacott of Thornworthy, Chagford, who has had sheep on the moor for fifty years has lost sixteen since the middle of July. Mr Wonnacott continues 'I've a neighbour who had about 140 sheep. He used to lose about twenty every year and when there were only twenty left, he sold them and finished with it.'

Mr Tom Pollard of Beestor, North Bovey, who has lost twenty sheep, said he would normally expect to lose four or five out of every hundred on the moor but would put that number down to natural wastage.

The article continued with the theory that these huge losses of stock were the result of sheep-rustling. Certainly rustling does occur. Hill-grazing stock is rounded up at night, loaded into lorries and transported to markets in other parts of the country where the animals are sold and slaughtered before their legitimate owners have become aware they have gone missing. But there could be other causes for the substantial losses of hill sheep. One was suggested four years later when the *Western Morning News* published an article with the headline 'The Black Beast Strikes Once More'.

Reports of big cats being seen on the moors had been made for years. Even a paper written on an archaeological dig on Dartmoor in the 1930s mentioned a puma-size cat seen by an archaeologist near one excavation site. The authorities seldom took such reports seriously. One policeman, the late Police Sergeant John Duckworth, did keep note of sightings in the Mid-Devon area out of personal interest. Other members of the police force have officially recorded their own sightings. Among them was Police Constable Farquharson, who was riding with the Mid-Devon Hunt in the Moretonhamstead area in February 1980 when the hounds put up a golden brown cat the size of a Labrador dog. He thought it could have been a puma.

It was definitely not a puma that was seen by his colleague, Police Constable Norris when, together with other police officers and members of the local fire brigade, he was called to a barn fire near Tedburn St Mary and spotted a black leopard-size cat on the hillside behind the farm.

At once the question arises: if exotic cats have been roaming Devon for years, why have none ever been killed? Surely if there were as many as people have claimed, some of them would have come to grief at the hands of their only predator – man. The moors might be wild but they are populated around the fringes and annually attract vast numbers of holidaymakers during the summer months.

After the publication early in 1983 of my book *Cat Country*, in which I suggested that a number of big cat reports from all over the British Isles should be linked, and that they appeared to be of an animal so far unrecorded in the zoological text books, I received hundreds of letters from members of the public, many claiming to have seen mystery cats. One elderly lady wrote to me from South Devon to say that when her husband had been a gamekeeper on a Dartmoor estate during the 1930s he had discovered one night a puma-size grey cat attacking the pheasants in the breeding pens. The cat had been cornered inside the run and shot, her husband simply disposing of the carcase as carrion bait. The lady deeply regretted that her husband was no longer alive to confirm her story, but she assured me that the animal had been the size of a leopard and grey in colour.

In 1963 Mr Richard Frost was out shooting rabbits with his brother-in-law near Swincome, not far from Hexworthy, when they put up a cat the size of a Labrador dog and shot it. Worried they had broken the law and killed either someone's

6

exotic pet, or else a protected animal, they buried t and said nothing about the incident for years.

If few people roam the moors with a gun, the great of carcases littering the roads during the summer testify to a more lethal weapon, the motor car. Deer, hill sheep, foxes, badgers, hares and hedgehogs all suf death penalty when they fall foul of the metallic mon number of witnesses have claimed to have seen the cats driving across the moors, and on at least two occasions suggested that the encounters had involved a collision w unidentified animal.

The first account I came across was of an accident rep by a member of the staff of Devonair Radio Station while driving at night across the moors with his father, startled by two black animals that darted out in front of car. One was struck and thrown on to the grass verge by impact. Shocked by the incident, and thinking that they have killed a dog, they stopped and got out of the car to se the animal was dead and not lying injured. Whatever they hit was certainly not dead. It snarled with such ferocity t they decided, injured or not, they were taking no chances a drove off. The next morning they returned to the spot daylight to find that the animal had gone, despite the injuri it must have received in the accident.

The only description they could give was of large, fast ar dark animals the size of big dogs. When the two men had g out of the car, they could see only two black shapes, the whit fangs highlighted as the creatures snarled and the eyes blazin in the glow from the car headlights. The most terrifying par of the encounter, however, was the sound the animals made Whatever they were, their behaviour appeared to be mor frightening than would be expected from even a large injured dog.

Another motorist and his wife were able to describe the animal they hit in daylight on the outskirts of Tedburn St Mary. The couple were holidaymakers who stumbled into

7

dismissed as public imagination, hoaxes or cases of mistaken identity.

The saga of the Surrey puma was perhaps the most famous and best documented of the British big cat hunts. The first reports of puma-size cats came in the 1950s from around the Surrey-Hampshire border, but it was not until the early 1960s that the police began to take the sightings seriously. The sudden official interest was probably due to the fact that police officers were among the numerous witnesses coming forward. Earlier, in the 1930s, the search for the Epping Forest lion had caused a stir, and armed police were in pursuit of a black panther-like sheep-killer in the Bettyhill area of Sutherland in 1976. In that same year police marksmen were also patrolling areas on the outskirts of Nottingham, looking for lionlike cats.

Not until my book *Cat Country* was published in February 1983 did the public and the media become aware, for the first time, of the huge volume of reports of unidentified cats across the whole of the British Isles. At that time, a number of new witnesses came forward, both to myself and to the media, and suddenly their sightings were taken seriously. Big cat hunting in Britain was no longer treated as a joke.

1

Death on the Moors

Every year hill farmers lose a small percentage of ewes and lambs, most to natural causes, though some to the occasional attack by rogue dogs, or even foxes. Britain long ago lost all its major natural predators. Where once the cave lion, the leopard, the cheetah and the wolf roamed the hills and moorlands, feeding off the native herd animals, man developed his intensive farming and industrialisation, interrupting the food chain and destroying the natural habitat on which the large predators depended. The last wild wolves in the British Isles were killed in the eighteenth century, and after that farmers could relax their guard over their grazing flocks as the largest wild predators remaining were the wildcat, the fox, and the badger, none of which posed a serious threat to stock.

A small number of sheep have always been lost to uncontrolled domestic dogs, and because of the carnage even small, normally placid pet dogs can cause to a flock, farmers are allowed to shoot any unattended dogs found among their animals. Foxes are also on the farmers' hit list. Although not powerful enough to attack a healthy ewe, a few foxes certainly do attack and kill newborn or weak lambs. The Scottish wildcat, *Felis silvestris silvestris*, and the largest British bird of prey, the golden eagle, are also known to attack young lambs, but both these predators are protected by law and farmers are forced to accept occasional losses to these species.

It was certainly neither Scottish wildcats nor eagles that were attacking lambs on the Devon farm of Eric Ley during the spring of 1982. He considered his flock to be the target of a fox, or a group of foxes, when night after night his lambs were killed and eaten. He shot a number of foxes, but whether he accounted for the culprit or the killing just stopped because the lambs grew larger and stronger he had no way of knowing. The loss of healthy lambs was annoying but part of the hazards of farming. As with climatic conditions and pest invasion, farmers have always accepted that some years are plentiful and others disastrous. Eric Ley hoped that 1983 would be a good year and make up for his present problems. Never, in his worst nightmare, could the quietly-spoken Devon farmer have anticipated what lay ahead.

In the following spring the killing began again and by April he had lost thirty lambs on his 180-acre farm, situated on the southern fringe of Exmoor near South Molton. Although such losses are not unknown when two or more dogs run amok in a flock, these killings were different. The predator struck at night, silently and swiftly, usually without appearing to disturb the rest of the flock that grazed around the killing site. The only evidence of the attack was the discovery of the remains of the victim the following morning, often no more than the skin, head, feet and backbone. Smaller lambs were sometimes carried away altogether, agitated ewes searching for their lost young the only indication that anything unusual had occurred in the night.

Eric Ley was not the only farmer to suffer losses in the spring of 1983. His neighbours were also reporting visits from the unseen predator. Together they took it in turns to patrol the fields at night, hoping for a clean shot to end the career of the unknown killer. Spring is always a difficult time for farmers involved in lambing and calving. Most grazing animals choose the cool dark hours of night in which to give birth, and in addition to their normal workload farmers spend night after night in the lambing-pen or cowshed, often with only a couple of hours of sleep over a period of several days. Already exhausted, the South Molton farmers did not want to spend their valuable rest hours patrolling the Devon hills, but they had no choice.

By the middle of April Eric Ley was facing a financial loss of more than £1,000 and the mystery predator was becoming more ambitious. Attacks were beginning to take place on fully-grown ewes, the victims usually killed by a throat bite and broken neck. The flesh was stripped from the chest down and inwards. With the situation out of control, the farmers called in the police. A group of fifty armed men, some mounted on horseback for easy movement across the rough countryside, supervised by the police and supported by a police helicopter, set out with the pack of Torrington Foot Beagles on the 19th April to search for the beast of Exmoor. The hunt lasted all day but the searchers were frustrated, missing their quarry despite the fact that the killer struck in daylight in the area being quartered.

If the hunters were unable to flush out the predator, others were reporting sightings of a strange beast. Seventeen-year-old Susan Fernandez was driving to work when she spotted an animal near Sannacott and Limeslake farms. She described it as large, black and catlike, with white feet and a long sweeping tail. A local bus driver, John Franks, described an animal he had seen ahead of him in a lane. 'It was broad in the beam, about two feet. Its jet black coat gleamed as though the thing had just stepped out of the hairdresser's. It was about 2 feet 6 inches to the shoulders and had powerful legs. I remember thinking God, but you're ugly. The head just didn't fit on the body. It was old with grey streaks running back from its muzzle and a mass of whiskers. It didn't seem to have a neck, just this squat head stuck on the end of its body.'

If this animal was difficult to recognise from Mr Franks's description, the creature described by farmer Maurice Knowles in April 1982 had been even harder to identify. He spotted the strange beast in his field at Ingleford, near Lydford, at 3 a.m. while he was checking his lambing ewes by spotlight. The beam revealed a black animal like a greyhound, about four or five feet long, snuffling its way along the hedgerow. He claimed it had a colt-like face and its eyes did not appear to reflect the light of his lamp.

March of 1983 produced a daylight sighting of a large catlike animal. Alan Trump, an Oxford University librarian, reported seeing the strange beast in bluebell woods near Ide, outside Exeter. He said, 'I only saw it from about 100 yards but it was a most peculiar creature.' Mr Trump, like Mr Knowles, seemed unable to give a clear identifiable description of the animal he had seen.

By the end of April Eric Ley and his neighbours were getting desperate as the attacks increased in ferocity. Powerless to stop the destruction of their stock, they were joined on their nightly patrols by police officers with night sights. Sergeant Dave Goodman at the South Molton police station said, 'Mr Ley is at his wits' end. He's tried everything he can.'

The hunt had begun to assume an aura of unreality as armed police and civilians searched the darkness, jumping at shadows, attempting to protect the peacefully grazing flocks from whatever it was that killed so swiftly and silently across the countryside. Yet, despite the manpower ranged against it, the mystery predator continued to attack and was suspected of killing about fifty sheep in a six-week period, its hunting ground a seven mile stretch of South Molton countryside around Eric Ley's farm.

The police were baffled. A spokesman appealed to local farmers to report any loss of livestock to Barnstaple police station. They hoped to be able to pinpoint the routes being used by the beast.

Following the appeal two building workers came forward to report having seen a large black panther-like creature near Whitcott Farm two years previously.

On 21st April a front-page story appeared in a North Devon newspaper reporting the hunt for an unknown predator killing sheep around South Molton. The following day the national newspapers picked up the story and the media circus began.

The press had got wind of another saga like that of the Surrey Puma. That a puma, or pumas, could have escaped and be living successfully feral in the English countryside was highly probable. Pumas are weak-jawed and non-aggressive animals, small and appealing when young and easily house trained. They became popular pets in the 1950s and 1960s. Like big dogs, many were purchased on a whim, as a novelty, without consideration of their needs as adult animals.

Some experts went so far as to suggest that the whole story was invented by a bored press during the so-called silly season! But if the media rejoiced in a new cat-hunt in the British countryside, the unfortunate Devon farmers were less than delighted by their sudden elevation to fame. Despite the continual armed patrols, they were finding more and more of their flocks at dawn reduced to bloody skeletons, sometimes up to 60lbs of meat being stripped from the carcases overnight. Bemused Ministry of Agriculture officials examined the resulting carnage and shook their heads. It had to be dogs, but what sort of dogs? And how many? Surely one rogue animal could not account for so much mutton being consumed in such a relatively short time.

Already a number of wandering dogs had been shot in the area, some obviously guilty of sheep-worrying. Others were simply innocent of any crime other than an unsupervised stroll along the country lanes. Bereaved dog-owners bitterly accused farmers of shooting anything that moved. Farmers in turn defended their shotgun activities by pointing to the dead sheep carcases littering the countryside, some of which undoubtedly had been attacked by domestic dogs. It was suggested that a number of personal feuds were being settled by the shooting of neighbours' pets.

Yet, despite the disposal of dogs and foxes, the beast kills continued as night after night the mystery predator dined off the local sheep. At the end of April the police gave a press conference at which Assistant Chief Constable Rupert Ormerod said that the killing was out of control and the Devon force was baffled as to the identity of the predator. He told the media that he was requesting help from the Royal Marine Commandos based at nearby Lympstone.

To have taken such an unusual and drastic step was some indication of how seriously the police were taking the attacks. The idea of calling in the highly-trained commandos to hunt down a rogue dog seemed to suggest panic measures, and few could believe that such a move would be considered unless there was a serious risk to the public. It seemed doubtful that any dog, unless suspected of carrying rabies, could warrant such an extreme measure. The locals began to suggest that a stray dog was not the identity of the mystery killer.

And if not a dog, then what was it?

The rumours of big cat sightings began to grow as more and more people claimed to have seen large black panther-size cats roaming the Devon countryside.

The kills were examined and the method of the animal's dispatch was carefully studied. The smaller lambs were often decapitated or had their skulls or rib cages crushed, as if by a large and powerful bite. The adult sheep showed bite and claw marks under the fleece and usually had their necks broken and their throats torn in a typical cat kill fashion. It was also noted that an attack was usually against just one animal and was so swift and complete that, as one vet observed, the speed of death had resulted in a total absence of bruising despite the horrendous injuries. Attacks by dogs are normally messy and usually involve more than one victim. Two or more dogs, working together as a pack, will go chasing and biting in play that develops into bloodlust.

The Exmoor beast kills were different – one animal targeted, dispatched and devoured swiftly, silently and cleanly.

My book *Cat Country*, published less than three months earlier, was constantly cited by the media. Some sceptics actually suggested the whole episode was one organised by the publishers as free publicity for the book. Had it been possible, it certainly would have been the publicity campaign of all campaigns.

The word cat began to be used openly by the media, and not only by the more sensational papers. The *Farming News* carried a front-page story on the 6th May under the banner headline 'Hunt for Killer Cat'. There was no suggestion that the predator might be a dog, or dogs. The report said that:

> North Devon farmers were tightlipped this week about the killer cat which has taken 50 sheep over the past six weeks. The large animal – believed to be a puma – hunts only at night. It has been known to kill and carry off lambs without disturbing the rest of the flock or watching farmers. Now a detachment of Royal Marines with night vision equipment is helping police track down the animal.

It is surprising that a farming publication would ignore the possibility of the culprit being a rogue dog, which is normally the immediate suspect when a sheep is found savaged on farmland. But farmers were used to the carnage resulting from dog-attacks and they knew that the carcases being discovered by their unfortunate Devon colleagues were not in keeping with the familiar pattern of dog kills. The police remained unconvinced by the farmers' arguments. Dogs frequently kill sheep, they reasoned, and so the obvious culprit for the South Molton attacks had to be a large and powerful wild dog. There was even speculation as to the combination of breeds that could inflict the terrible injuries found on the victims.

Charles Trevisick, a former Ilfracombe zoo-owner, backed the police theory. He suggested that the attacker was a feral bitch with pups. He said, 'When the pups are about eight weeks old they will show themselves and reveal the hideout of the mother.' The farmers were not holding their breath in anticipation of that event.

Dr Henry Durston-Smith, the owner of Burwell Farm, where Susan Fernandez had reported seeing a strange catlike creature, said: 'The pattern is always the same. The lamb is dispatched very silently and suddenly. If it were a dog or fox, the ewes would be all in one corner, but they don't move and don't seem to know it's gone. He's obviously killing for food not mayhem. It's got to be wiped out somehow or other. Somebody is keeping quiet about it, because I think it belongs to one of these people who keep exotic animals in their back garden.'

The publicity was getting out of hand. The only thing that the farmers and the authorities could agree upon was that the marauder had to be wiped out!

Farmers were now facing heavy financial losses and the police, by their claims that the killer was a rogue dog, appeared to be unable to control a simple case of sheep worrying. It was in such a highly charged atmosphere at the end of April that Sergeant Major Andy Wilkins of the Royal Marine Commandos, together with a corporal, arrived quietly at Drewstone Farm for a recce to assess the situation.

Although parts of Dartmoor are used by the commandos as a training ground, the rough bleak terrain being ideal for cross-country forced marches and survival exercises, the use of firearms is totally prohibited except on the firing ranges set aside for the discharge of live ammunition. Even to consider using armed forces personnel to patrol the Devonshire countryside during peacetime was an extraordinary step to take. Attempting to fire a rifle in a civilian area posed enormous problems for the marines. To take such drastic measures against a dog or dogs (the official story) made the decision to call in the Royal Marine Commandos without precedent. It was little wonder that the national media took more than a passing interest in the events unfolding on the once peaceful Devon moorlands.

The farmers welcomed the coming of the marines like civilians welcoming friendly forces in a war zone. They were weary and frustrated, and the losses of their stock were increasing at an alarming rate. The creature or creatures responsible for the carnage seemed unstoppable, almost supernatural. No one felt safe from the constant threat, and there was always the unvoiced fear – first lambs, then fully grown sheep; would the beast tire of mutton and start to look for other prey?

As one farmer put it glumly, 'You'd need a pack of bloody Great Danes to eat that much, and then they'd be going some!'

After Sergeant Major Andy Wilkins had talked to Eric Ley he felt sorry for the softly spoken Devon farmer and his young wife. Ruth Ley told him that another lamb had been attacked but had survived the ordeal despite horrific injuries. The lamb had been completely scalped, the skin on its head, including its ears, ripped off, exposing the bone of the skull. One side of the face was laid bare to the cheek-bone, the eye torn from its socket. It was difficult to believe the attack had been made by a dog, for the injuries appeared to have been caused by ripping, not a biting action. It was as if the lamb had received a side swipe from a massive clawed paw, a glancing blow that had not been followed up with a mortal strike. It was amazing that the lamb had survived such injuries. It was certainly living proof of the power and ferocity of its attacker.

An experienced hunter, tracker and sniper instructor, the Sergeant Major felt confident that his men could trap the attacker, whatever it was, and end its reign of terror. It was not the first time that the Royal Marine Commandos, like other members of the armed forces, had received a request for assistance from the police – though usually it was to help in the search for a missing person or to deal with a natural disaster, such as a flood. The idea that the police would officially request military help to deal with a situation involving sheep killing had to be without parallel.

Sergeant Major Wilkins said, 'At the farmhouse we met a large group of people, including local farmers and land-owners, a white hunter from Kingsteignton, a police super-intendent from Barnstaple and Sergeant Dave Goodman from South Molton police. There were lengthy discussions about what the beast was and it was fairly obvious to me that catching it was of minor consideration as opposed to who was right about the identity of the beast, whether it was a rogue dog, some sort of feral cat or even a galloping pig, as it was suggested at one stage!'

The two marines were shown round the area and spent the night without seeing anything of the mystery predator. They returned to Lympstone to report to Major Watkins that there was indeed a problem and that the marines could probably be of assistance.

On 1st May Sergeant Major Wilkins collected a group of men together. They zeroed in their weapons, adjusting the sights to each individual marksman for maximum precision. Then, with various stores and equipment, they made their way to Drewstone Farm.

The Sergeant Major recalled, 'We arrived there late in the afternoon and set up camp in a large cattleshed which had held bullocks throughout the winter and was eighteen inches deep in straw and muck. Eric Ley had bulldozed a space for us, divided off with straw bales, where we set up our camp beds and sleeping-bags. Around us were penned lambing ewes and it was fairly noisy.'

The noise was unimportant as the sleeping-bags were to remain largely unoccupied for the first part of the campaign. When they had unloaded their stores and organised their living quarters, the marines met a police superintendent who explained the restrictions under which they would be operating. One police officer would be with them at all times. The marines would not be allowed to fire their weapons unless they were aiming downhill. This was to ensure there was a natural backdrop for the bullets to strike if they missed their target. There was to be no firing at all in the direction of any houses.

'At this stage the police were treating the whole situation with an odd attitude,' Andy Wilkins commented. 'I think they were all worried about releasing a group of trained killers into the countryside, frightened that we were going to rape all the women and put curses on their unborn children. The average civilian in the area had no idea what the marines were or did. I think they were all working with Second World War notions, when Churchill was accused by Hitler of releasing thieves and murderers from prison and turning them into commandos. Hitler had actually put out an order that all captured commandos were to be shot immediately after being interrogated. They weren't to be classed as ordinary soldiers because they were criminals.'

It is doubtful that the police were actually afraid of what the marines might do but they must have been worried about losing control of the situation to the military.

A problem arose almost immediately. PC Martin Abbot arrived only to discover that the police radio was incompatible with theirs. This meant that one marine with a radio had to remain with the policeman at all times, relaying the information from the marines to PC Abbot, who in turn would pass the information on to police headquarters. This reduced the marine manpower by one marksman, and with such a large area of countryside to cover, Andy Wilkins could little afford the loss of even one sniper. The remaining marines were organised into pairs to work from positions which were changed daily in the light of information concerning the movements of the beast collected the previous night.

Operation Beastie, as the hunt was code-named, was about to begin. No one, civilian or military, could anticipate what lay ahead, although the marines presumed they would be in the area for no more than a couple of days. That should be time enough to track down the mystery killer, dispose of it and then pull out before the media became aware of their presence. The operation was to be swift, silent and professional. It was only a matter of time, hours with luck, days at the most, before the unknown attacker would be stretched out dead in Eric Ley's yard and the whole episode closed.

From Barnstaple Chief Inspector Roy Roberts hastened to reassure the public that, if the marines were involved, they would not be operating under a shoot on sight policy. Their primary objective would be to capture the animal alive. Both farmers and marines smiled at the senior police officer's statement. The real objective was to stop the killing by any means necessary. There was just one obvious way in which to do that, and they intended to do it at the first opportunity.

The day after the marines' arrival at Drewstone I turned up to interview Eric and Ruth Ley, as arranged previously, only to be told that if I wished to talk to the men I would have to wait as they were sleeping.

'What men?' I asked, unaware of the decision to call in the marines.

I found myself in a difficult situation. When I met Sergeant Major Wilkins he made it obvious that he did not want me around. He had been told I was a crank, with some outrageous theory about unknown big cats roaming the countryside, but the area was not under military rule and that made it difficult for him to order me away. On the other hand, like the farmers, I felt that if anyone could succeed in putting an end to the beast of Exmoor, then the marines were the people to do it. If there was to be a kill, and the predator turned out to be a cat, then I wanted to be present when it happened, to examine the carcase for myself.

I defied the unwelcome glares and invited myself along for the fun, setting up camp in the barn alongside the men.

The news that the marines had arrived to hunt the beast broke in the press the following day. At first these were just small interest items printed, but as the idea of armed élite forces patrolling the Devonshire countryside caught the public's imagination so it turned into a media romp.

The police attempted to control the civilian side of the hunt, keeping the numerous reporters and sightseers out of the area. As if in a war zone, Drewstone Farm was suddenly sealed off from the outside world.

A pattern appeared to be forming to the beast's nocturnal killing, with a victim every two or three days being partly devoured. Other deaths were reported in the area but these were suspected to be dog kills or deaths from natural causes. Some kills were far from natural, with necks broken, fleeces peeled back, throats frequently ripped open and a quantity of meat stripped from the carcases.

As the media descended on South Molton, the beast hysteria spread across North Devon and Somerset. Witnesses talked openly of sightings of strange black beasts seen over the years. To the delight of the press, many described large panther-size creatures, definitely feline in appearance, but others gave confusing accounts, attempting to describe creatures that seemed to have a combination of both canine and feline features.

It was clear that some descriptions were the work of overactive imagination, or even of whimsical invention; others were the result of illusion, or error, genuine mistaken identity. Even so, the police were impressed by the sincerity of some witnesses who claimed clear, sometimes daylight sighting of creatures they could describe with no hint of confusion but could not match exactly to any known animal, canine or feline.

The authorities were mystified, the inhabitants of the area frightened, and the media had a field day.

The Royal Marine Commandos ignored the surrounding hysteria and, shouldering their rifles, set out simply to complete a task to stop the sheep killing. The beast might have run rings around the civilian farmers and country police officers but now it faced the professionals! The beast's days were obviously numbered and farmers could sleep in peace, knowing their grazing flocks had the ultimate protection.

Yet, despite the odds, and the forces raised against it, the beast of Exmoor killed on.

And on.

And on!

2

Media and Marines

If people were worried about being attacked when walking alone through beast country, and farmers were despairing of the financial ruin that the mystery creature was going to cause them, the media loved the beast of Exmoor with a deep and sincere devotion. The local newspapers began the circus with small stories about strange cats being sighted and farmers facing sheep losses, but soon the local press was swept aside as the national newshounds arrived in a pack. The once peaceful market-town of South Molton was suddenly invaded by hard-news men wielding credit cards and cameras, some of whom had experienced the major trouble spots of the world. It was a bewildering and interesting time for those locals who were not directly affected by the beast's activities. The hotels were full to overflowing, the pubs were crowded and car-hire firms did a roaring trade, ferrying customers round to the spots where the most recent sightings had occurred.

With the arrival of the Royal Marines, the region began to be divided into war zones, the police barricading the area where the marines were operating in an attempt to keep away the media and idle voyeurs. The precautions were sensible. It was obvious that too many feet stamping around the countryside would alert the predator that it was under surveillance and it would change its territory, making it more difficult to track. More important was the fear of an outsider accidentally coming under sniper fire. The marines were using SLR's with image intensifiers, rifles that could put a bullet through a solid brick wall and could kill a man within a range of 2,500 metres. The greatest fear was of a member of the public moving around in the darkness, in the sights of the marines' guns. As one harassed and worried marine put it, 'We're out to get whatever is killing the sheep, but in the dark it's hard to distinguish the sheep themselves from whatever is preying on them. We don't want the added complication of trying to work out if it's a sheep's bum or a bloody civilian's stuck up in the air, crawling around the undergrowth!'

Unfortunately a number of the media personnel did not appreciate the very real danger involved and constantly attempted to breach the barriers and enter the surveillance area in the hope of achieving the first film of the beast, dead or alive. Some reporters considered it well worth an uncomfortable night wriggling through the South Molton bushes in the hope of an 'exclusive'.

At first the marines refused to have any dealings with the media, but as the pressures increased, so the media became more demanding and it was decided to hold a press conference in an attempt to satisfy the reporters' curiosity and encourage them to stay out of the search area. Because of their connection with other trouble spots, and the obvious clandestine nature of their activities working undercover, the marines organised a press meeting using only marines that were either shortly due to leave the force or else were willing to face the cameras heavily disguised. Festooned with camouflage netting and twigs that completely obscured their faces, they hoped to avoid recognition by any interested parties.

The media was impressed with the window-dressing.

Those actually involved in the hunt sniggered at the sight of the concealed marines. Camouflage might have had a valid use in an area where enemy snipers were watching for the shape of a man, but a wild animal relying on scent and sound was hardly going to be impressed or warned off by the marines' transformed appearance. The whole scene was a farce, set up purely for the media.

Andy Wilkins and one other member of the group wandered self-consciously along the lane under the scrutiny of press and television cameras and settled in a ditch, their rifles poised menacingly, aimed for an imaginary beast in the nearby bushes. The remainder of the marines stayed hidden in the farm shed that was being used as a base, attempting to grab a couple of hours sleep or cleaning their weapons, after a night out in sniper positions. Ruth Ley and I were also keeping a low profile, ignoring the activities outside the shed and feeding the orphaned lambs, some of whose mothers had fallen prey to the beast.

Suddenly the country sound of singing birds and bleating sheep was broken by a sharp piercing crack, the unmistakable report of a single rifle shot.

At once everyone hidden in the shed was awake and alert. Had the beast actually made an appearance in daylight before the world's press or had there been a terrible accident? The only guns out of the shed were those carried by the two marines being filmed and the Major who was actually giving the interview. All three men were sensible and responsible, it was inconceivable that any of them would fire their weapons with so many civilians in the area.

The immediate fear was that there had been an accident. Perhaps a marine had slipped and involuntarily discharged his weapon, or had the beast been spotted during the filming and the marines taken the opportunity to have a crack at it?

A more sinister possibility was that it was not one of the marines who had fired the gun but another marksman, possibly a terrorist, who had used the press conference as cover for a lightning attack.

Everyone in the shed waited in suspense for the return of the Sergeant Major. If he was going to return.

When finally he appeared, furiously mouthing obscenities about idiots who discharged guns for no reason, it transpired that Major Watkins, who had been standing behind the two men posing for cameras in a ditch, had responded to questions about their weapons with a demonstration. He had shot a crow.

Andy Wilkins was not amused. 'We were hidden in the ditch when we heard the shot and we both pissed our pants thinking the other had accidently discharged his weapon straight at the bloody civilians.' No harm had been done but it was an example of the difficulties involved in Operation Beastie. The media demanded the rights of a free press to have access to information about a situation that obviously could not be covered by the Official Secrets Act and the marines felt they could not do their job properly with the civilians under their feet.

A 'them-and-us' situation had already developed and the farmers, afraid that the marines would be forced to pull out and desert them, began to feud openly with the media. There were a number of incidents in which farmers, finding media people on their land, threatened violence if reporters and television crews did not get off their property.

The police tried to calm the situation, acting as mediators between the opposing parties. It was a hopeless task. Farmers wanted the beast dead and their stock protected, the marines wanted to get on with their job quietly, and the media wanted to keep the headlines blazing as the whole country and the rest of the world watched the activities of the beast hunters with fascination.

Beast hysteria began to grip the whole of the British Isles. Thousands of people reported sightings of mystery cats in other areas and well-meaning people as well as cranks offered advice.

Both the police and the marines in Devon received

instructions from their seniors. Don't speculate to the press about what the beast might be, and don't mention cats of any size, large or small. 'You are hunting a rogue dog.'

It was in this atmosphere of distrust and cover-up that one marine (I shall call him John) spotted a large black beast walking along the disused railway line near Drewstone farm. He watched the animal through his night sights for a few minutes but was unable to shoot for fear of hitting a farmhouse that was in his direct line of fire. It was frustrating for the marksman. The beast was in range, one shot could finish its reign of terror for good and the marines could leave the circus and return to their own world away from the glare of publicity, doing the job for which they were trained – the protection of their country.

As it was, the beast's luck held, and the watching marine let it pass unsuspecting out of range. It was the first time that the marines had had a look at what they were actually hunting, and from that moment they began to mention among themselves the word cat.

When the men returned from their sniper positions, John described what he had seen. He said it was a large, powerfully-built, black catlike animal, unlike anything else he had ever seen. Coming off duty, just a short time after the sighting, he was certain that the creature was not a breed of dog. Yet a couple of hours later he suddenly changed his story. He claimed he had seen a huge, powerful black doglike animal padding along the railway line. It was obvious, though, that he was uncomfortable with the new version of his sighting.

Privately, there was now dissension between the police officers and the marines themselves. Some believed the official line that the beast was obviously a large rogue dog but others had seen the carnage, if not the attacker, and they could not accept that any dog, of whatever breed, could produce the type of injuries seen on the victims. John's original version of his sighting only increased their belief that the beast was not a dog, whatever the official statement.

Dog or cat, the beast seemed more than a match for its experienced and highly-trained hunters. Every night the marines slipped quietly into pre-arranged sniper positions where they settled down to watch over the peaceful lanes and fields of South Molton. Each morning they trudged back wearily to breakfast and attempted to grab a couple of hours' sleep before tracking through the surrounding countryside, following up the most recent reports and deciding the following night's sniper positions. Every couple of days they returned to be faced with yet another beast kill. It seemed sometimes as if the beast were watching them, following their every move and striking when it wished, always behind their positions and out of range of their rifles.

And the media followed the hunt with dedication, the controversy still raging across the country as to the identification of the beast.

Then, after the first unsuccessful week of the hunt, the tired marines and police officers received some disquieting news. The *Daily Express* was taking an initiative in the beast hunt and offered a reward of £1,000 for the beast, dead or alive!

The official hunters were horrified. Such publicity might increase the sales of the newspapers, but the idea of treasure hunters roaming the moors, taking pot shots at anything that moved, was disturbing, to say the least, and for the whole charade to be taking place under the snipers' guns was an impossible situation for the police and the marines.

An outcry was raised against the cheap publicity stunt. The police called the *Daily Express* bounty a licence for any amateur gun to go roaming the moors, and the result was almost certain to be hunters shooting each other. Animal rights movements and the RSPCA objected to the obvious risk to other livestock on the moors, claiming that the *Daily Express* offer would result in wholesale slaughter of wild animals and farm stock.

The *Daily Express* took the point that it was irresponsible to encourage unskilled guns on the moors but they refused to withdraw the reward. Instead they agreed to alter the offer to shooting with a camera rather than with a gun. The £1,000 reward was now to be awarded for the best photograph taken of the beast, whatever its identification. The change of rules obviously lessened the risk but did not remove it entirely. After all, a dead animal was going to be a lot easier to photograph than a live one, and, supposing the creature to be something like a panther, a number of the unofficial hunters were going to be armed with more than a camera before they were willing to set foot on to beast territory. And if unauthorised guns were a headache for the local police, the thought of civilians wandering around in front of their weapons was even more disturbing for the marine officers.

Andy Wilkins commented, 'We need to be left alone in silence to stand a chance of killing the animal. We are dealing with a wild predator. We have to sit perfectly still in hedges and hiding places from dusk till dawn to get a chance to kill. We haven't got a hope if photographers are stumbling around all over the place.'

The official marine spokesman said, 'It's too dangerous to carry on. We could be inundated with bounty hunters in front of our rifle sights.'

On the Saturday morning after the *Daily Express* had made the reward offer, groups of police officers, farmers and weary marines stood around the yard of Drewstone Farm, waiting for instructions. Andy was called to the phone in the house. When he emerged again, he shook his head unhappily.

'We're pulling out!' he announced angrily.

The cavalier behaviour of the *Daily Express* had forced the Colonel to the conclusion that the continued involvement of the marines would put the public at risk. The professionals were returning to base, leaving despairing farmers and bewildered police officers to cope with the situation.

The marines were bitter that their hard work, loss of sleep and uncomfortable conditions of the past days had all been for nothing. The farmers were furious that the press had caused their only hope of protecting their livestock to be snatched from them. The police had no idea how to cope with the highly charged emotions of a situation that seemed to be rapidly getting out of control.

The *Daily Express* was unrepentant, claiming that:

> An orchestrated storm in a teacup was whipped up at the weekend over the Express's offer of £1,000 reward for a picture of the mysterious 'big cat' which has apparently been killing lambs in the Exmoor area.
>
> Local police chief Superintendent Douglas McClary is quoted as saying that public safety had been 'put at risk' by the Express offer. We find this astonishing.
>
> We spoke to Superintendent McClary on Friday. What he said then was, 'I see nothing against a reward.'

The paper claimed to have consulted the marines who had said they were hunting the beast only at night. Consequently the *Daily Express* had considered a warning to readers not to hunt at night as sufficient to prevent the public wandering around the countryside under the noses of the armed marines.

If the *Express* claimed that their offer had police approval, they admitted that they did not have the farmers' support.

> We spoke to local farmers and landowners who told us they were worried that an influx of amateur photographers might lead to crops being damaged and animals frightened. So we warned readers not to trespass and strictly to observe the country code.

To suggest that all readers would take notice of the *Express*'s instruction when there was a race on to win £1,000 was naïve, to say the least. Neither the police nor the farmers took great comfort in their claim that their readers would obviously take heed of the paper's warnings. The highly-charged situation was not helped by the *Express* stating:

Anyone carrying firearms for whatever purpose has, of course, an over-riding duty to ensure that public safety is not put at risk.

This was true before and after the Daily Express reward offer.

No one – not even the Royal Marines – can avoid this responsibility.

It is only the irresponsible use of firearms and not so-called 'irresponsible journalism' which is likely to lead to people being killed or injured. No one who took the trouble to read our reward offer last Saturday could possibly accuse the Daily Express of irresponsible behaviour.

We wish we could say the same of some of our more hysterical critics.

The paper did not suggest how the marines could do their job and fire their guns to end the reign of terror when the monetary offer encouraged civilians to crawl around the sniper-covered countryside. Either they were free to fire or they were not. If not, there was no point in them sitting around night after night in water-filled ditches. After all, it needed only one *Daily Express* reader to decide that £1,000 was worth the risk, and to leap up in the sights of a marine as he pulled the trigger, to produce a tragedy, whether the misguided reader was carrying a gun or just a camera.

The editor of the *Daily Express* was named Sir Larry Lamb, and his hysterical critics, the farmers who night after night were finding their livestock ripped apart and eaten, continued to accuse the paper of irresponsible behaviour and suggested it might change his mind if he were to be tethered with his namesakes overnight in a South Molton field!

As the war of words continued and tempers frayed, the North Devon MP, Tony Speller, stepped into the conflict. 'I asked the *Daily Express* to withdraw their offer,' he said. 'The situation is getting desperate. But unfortunately they have decided to keep the reward on offer. As a result the Royal Marines have refused to resume their hunt until the publicity has died down. They can't operate with interruption.'

A spokesman for the Royal Marines confirmed Mr

Speller's statement. 'It's too dangerous to carry on. We could be inundated with bounty hunters in front of our rifle sights.'

Mr Speller contacted the Ministry of Agriculture for help for the furious farmers. 'This is something out of the ordinary and the problem must be resolved,' he said.

At least that was a sentiment everyone could agree upon. But the question was, how? With the marines gone, the carnage continued in the South Molton fields.

If nature in the form of the beast was causing the problem, she also helped to resolve the 'Reward' dilemma. A week after the marines pulled out, the heavens opened and torrential rain poured down over the mist-shrouded landscape, turning the lanes and fields to a morass of mud. Any amateur photographer, or marksman, visualising a happy sunny holiday on the moors, with the possible bonus of £1,000 spending money, rapidly went off the idea. A journalist surveyed the miserable scene and commented wryly, 'There are certainly no Bank Holiday-type jams around South Molton.'

Television crews from home and abroad clustered around in small groups, waiting for a break in the weather to allow filming. BBC's 'Nationwide' crew asked me to take part in a programme and I agreed willingly, welcoming the chance to add my voice to those condemning the *Express* offer. We managed to get some filming completed between the heavy showers but still needed a few more shots. Huddled in cars parked on a lane verge, we waited for the desperately needed break in the solid mass of grey clouds. A car containing two journalists pulled up alongside. I knew them both from past interviews. One of them, the *Daily Express* reporter, was terrified of being recognised by the locals and was living like a spy, undercover in enemy territory.

'It's all right for them back at the office,' he moaned bitterly. 'They aren't here, living in fear of their bloody lives!'

He agreed that the reward should have been withdrawn when its implications were realised, but unfortunately –

having made the bounty offer – the powers at the top refused to lose face and back down.

We left the poor man, huddled in his waterproof clothing, dreading discovery by an irate South Molton farmer and desperately wanting to be allowed to go home.

The *Express* reporter wasn't alone in inviting the anger of the locals. All the media personnel took stick as the hatred and fear of the mystery beast became focused on the representatives of the cause of the marines withdrawing. Some of this hatred took the form of general abuse or the cold shoulder, but reporters and film crews also came up against dislike in a more subtle form. The 'Nationwide' crew told me of one incident when they were interviewing farmers at the local market. With the cameras set up and running, the farmer being interviewed and smiling cheerfully at the camera suddenly farted loudly, ruining the sound-track. They tried again, only to be treated to a repeat performance, making the whole interview useless, the farmer not so much as blinking an eye as he chatted on.

The producer thought the incident was accidental and put it down to eccentric country yokel behaviour. I felt sure that the farmer's grin had not been one of innocence so much as one of satisfaction for a job well done.

Other farmers attempted to tackle the beast in their own way. The marines might have pulled out but the problem of protecting their stock remained. Following a sighting of a big black beast at Molland, a posse of thirty armed farmers immediately set off to sweep through the area. They searched the countryside from the Black Cock Inn to Crimson Cross but, as usual, the beast eluded them.

Denys Smaldon of the National Farmer's Union said, 'We eventually gave up when it got too dark to continue. What we really want is the Royal Marines to return. They are much better equipped to hunt at night. They have night sights, they are trained marksmen and trackers, and they have radio communication.'

The police agreed. A spokesman said, 'We are still trying to help the farmers track down this animal. Our only concern is for public safety and for people to stay away. This is a serious matter and we don't want to turn it into a circus. We want to get the situation back to normal and find this animal.'

It was doubtful if South Molton could return to normal after the events of the past weeks. To find the animal, searchers had to have a clearer idea of what they were looking for. Despite consultation with numerous experts, and the Ministry of Agriculture involvement, no one had yet put a positive identity on the mystery killer. Both marines and police statements, that they were sure the beast was simply a powerful rogue dog, drew doubting comments from many who were sceptical of the official version. Andy Wilkins believed they were hunting a dog, but then added that they had all heard wild and weird screams that could not be identified as coming from any sort of British wildlife. Even when the marines found dog hairs, and took a cast of what was identified as a dog's paw print from the scene of a beast sighting, a police spokesman, instead of claiming it as proof of their canine theory, remarked with strange reticence, 'It proves nothing.'

The local farmers were more positive. Denys Smalden said, 'It kills and eats lambs like no dog or fox ever did. It pulls wool away and attacks the shoulder and rump.' He added, 'It leaves the bone structure of the neck like you would leave a fishbone in a restaurant.'

The confusion was not lessened by the conflicting descriptions from witnesses claiming sightings of the mystery beast. Most described a beast the size of a black Labrador dog but with a flat catlike face, powerful build and long sweeping tail. Some described lurcher or mastiff cross-type dogs. Undoubtedly some of the creatures reported had no connection with the beast and were simply household pets taking unaccompanied walks or farm dogs roaming freely.

The exact number of kills credited to the Exmoor Beast was

also suspect. There was no doubt that the predator was responsible for a large number of kills, but moorland sheep die of various causes, some natural and others as a result of dog attacks or misadventure. In the May of 1983, however, every sheep carcase discovered was automatically claimed to be the work of the beast. Perhaps some were, but not all.

In an atmosphere of resentment, confusion and panic, the marines quietly returned to Drewstone Farm to attempt to finish the job they had started.

3

Other Hunts and Other Beasts

The feelings of frustration and helplessness felt by the farmers of South Molton were not without precedence. The earliest well-documented hunt for a mystery beast was the legendary pursuit of the Girt Dog of Ennerdale.

This creature first made its presence felt in the spring of 1810 when a Cumberland farmer discovered a dead and half-eaten ewe on the fells above Ennerdale Water. Other kills followed as night after night a mystery predator attacked the peacefully grazing flocks throughout the vale. Shepherds and farmers nightly patrolled the hills but the unseen killer seemed unstoppable as the first light of dawn continued to reveal the fresh carcases of the previous night's victims.

The farming community knew that such carnage could not be the work of foxes. A very large and powerful rogue dog in the area was judged to be the culprit but, despite all-night vigils on the hillsides and attempts to track the predator with packs of dogs, the desperate farmers had met their match. Whatever they were up against seemed to have extraordinary intelligence and cunning, never attacking the same flock on consecutive nights and successfully avoiding any contact with those pursuing it.

The hunting territory was very large if just one animal was responsible for the killings, for it attacked without warning both fell and valley flocks alike, leaving stripped carcases as calling cards to announce its visit.

Eventually, a shepherd patrolling his flock at dawn spotted the predator, but the sighting took the hunters no nearer to identifying the beast for it was unlike any other creature the shepherd had ever seen. He described it as a very large tawny-yellow animal like a lion, its smooth coat patterned with dark grey tiger stripes.

At market gatherings in the dales people argued about the identity of the killer. While some said it was a lion, others thought it was a cross between a mastiff and a greyhound. Still others gloomily swore that it was not an ordinary animal of flesh and blood but a supernatural beast, a hound of the Devil himself!

All the speculation and animated discussion did nothing, however, to protect the flocks from almost nightly raids. The beast travelled considerable distances with amazing speed, sometimes appearing to be in two places at the same time. It attacked swiftly and silently, leaving its trail of destruction to be discovered at dawn.

The hardy fell sheepdogs were a loyal courageous breed, used to protecting their charges against any danger and trained to obey their masters' commands instantly, but the Girt Dog – as the mystery assailant became known – had a devastating effect on them. Close proximity to the beast had them cowering in fright, too terrified to give chase if their quarry was nearby. The farmers put together a large pack of hunting-hounds and by the summer they were ready to hunt the Girt Dog down. With the pack on the scent, the tawny grey-striped beast suddenly broke cover and set off at great speed. Then, appearing to tire of the game, the creature turned to face its attackers. The leading hounds were dealt with instantly, the remaining dogs fleeing from the battle-field, leaving the farmers helpless and humiliated by the rout of their prize pack. The Girt Dog did not stay to enjoy its victory but, in the confusion, made a quick exit from the scene of the massacre.

Unwilling to lose any more good dogs, the farmers tried another tack. They littered the hillsides with poisoned carcases, but the Girt Dog had no interest in carrion when there was so much plump fresh mutton grazing the same slopes. The superstitious fears of the local folk were not lessened by the predator's taste for blood. Some kills were left with meat untouched but the blood lapped from the wound, vampire fashion.

As the whole countryside became gripped in a terror of the supernatural, substantial rewards were offered and local men carried their guns with them at all times in the hope of a lucky shot. The dales were full of tales of courage and near misses, but still the beast continued to deplete the grazing flocks of Ennerdale.

One man, Willy Jackson, reported suddenly coming face to face with the Girt Dog, finding it studying him calmly from a distance of only thirty yards. Willy bravely took a shot at the creature but the Girt Dog sloped off without a sound. An old man had an even closer encounter. Jack Wilson was very deaf and very old and bent, with legs so bowed 'you could run a wheelbarrow through 'em'. One day, while he was collecting firewood, his deafness prevented him hearing the approaching hunt, so he was unaware that thirteen men had closed in on the Girt Dog, cornering it in the adjoining cornfield. As the men aimed their guns towards the centre of the circle, the trapped beast made a sudden break for freedom, dashing towards a man named Will Rotherby. Will decided that discretion was the better part of valour, and with a scream of 'Skerse! What a dog!', he leapt sideways to safety. But old Jack, oblivious of all the excitement, had no such opportunity for escape. The Girt Dog headed straight for him, charged between his legs, tossing the old man into the air to land in a startled heap as the beast made good its escape.

Having recovered from the shock and the undignified somersault, old Jack swore for the rest of his life that the Girt Dog had been no dog, but a Girt Lion!

Dog or cat, the Girt Beast survived the encounter to continue its lethal raids on the dale's sheep. Experienced huntsmen were called in to join in the fray and the Girt Dog provided them with runs that became folklore in hunting circles. One run involving about two hundred riders set off early in the morning, the hounds picking up the scent on Kinniside Fell and chasing the quarry to Wastwater. From there the hunt continued to Calder, then to Seascale, before the chase had to be called off because of failing light.

The enthusiasm of the local inhabitants for the hunt can be judged by what happened on Sunday morning when the hounds gave cry near Ennerdale Church while a service was being conducted. As the howl of the scent being taken filled the church, every male member of the congregation was on his feet instantly and rushed outside to join in the chase, the parson himself among them. The Girt Dog led them to Cockermouth where the hunt came to an end in a violent thunderstorm, perhaps a judgement from above on the lack of respect for the Sunday service. On another day, after the Girt Dog had led the chase from Ennerdale to St Bees before the hunt had been abandoned, observers reported seeing the beast quietly following its pursuers as they trudged wearily back home.

It was the desperation and disappointment of the hunters of 1810 that the farmers of South Molton would have recognised and had sympathy with in 1983. But at least the 1810 beast saga had a successful conclusion. On 12th September of that year the Girt Dog was finally tracked down, surrounded and shot. Despite being badly injured, it managed to make a bid to escape in the direction of the River Enen where it was discovered cooling its wounds in the water. It made a last dash for freedom towards Eskat Woods, but there its luck ran out. The beast was flushed out of the trees and mortally wounded, the hunting dogs finally getting up enough courage to go in and finish it off. The Girt Dog was dead and a legend was born.

The identity of the beast was never confirmed, maybe because it had not been possible to recognise the creature once the hounds had finished with the body.

Over a hundred and seventy years and a few hundred miles separated the demise of the Girt Dog and the hunt for the Beast of Exmoor, but the similarities are striking – a mystery predator defying its armed and determined hunters, continually striking at will, swiftly and silently preying on grazing hill sheep. Despite reported glimpses of the creatures, no clear description emerged of either animal, even when encountered at close quarters. In both cases there were arguments as to identity, whether canine or feline? Both predators attacked over a wide area, sometimes appearing in two different locations at the same time, conjuring up a superstitious terror in the minds of many of those arrayed against them.

Records show that the Girt Dog's reign of terror lasted for just half a year before the predator, whatever its identity, was torn apart on the edge of Eskat Woods. Surely with modern technology, sophisticated weaponry and the skill of the Royal Marine Commandos, the reign of the Exmoor beast was destined to be of much shorter duration?

It was a comforting thought for farmers such as Eric Ley.

Yet, even with modern aids such as image intensifiers and night sights, searches for similar creatures in recent years – the Surrey Puma, for instance – had not been resolved successfully.

Chroniclers of the famous Surrey puma refer to *Rural Rides* by William Cobbett, published in 1830, as the first record of an unusual cat-sighting in the Surrey area. Cobbett describes seeing a spotted cat as big as a middle-size spaniel in the grounds of Waverley Abbey. The real saga began more than a century later, when a number of witnesses started to report large puma-like cats along the Surrey Hampshire border. These early sightings were treated as some sort of hoax and no records were kept until, in July 1962, Ernest Jellett, an employee of the Mid-Wessex Water Board, reported encountering a two-feet-high sandy-coloured cat on the North Downs at Farnham.

A number of other sightings followed Mr Jellett's, all of them taken seriously by the police, and the Surrey Puma hunt had begun in earnest. Many of the sightings were in the vicinity of Bushylease Farm at Condall where the farm manager, Mr Edward Blanks, and his family said they had seen three distinctly separate big cats. One was a large powerfully built tawny cat the size of a Great Dane, with darker reddish-brown shading along its back. A second animal was also sighted fairly frequently, similar in size and build to the brown animal but with a very dark grey or black coat. A third cat, seen only three times by the Blanks family but also reported by other witnesses, was smaller than the other two, about the size of a springer spaniel dog, ginger in colour with darker spots and thin stripes in its coat.

Other witnesses reported the same confusing variety of coloured cats and the police, no doubt influenced by some of their colleagues reporting sightings of brown puma-like cats, ignored any description that was not consistent with a North American puma. They reasoned that a puma could have escaped unreported or simply have been abandoned by an owner once the novelty of owning an exotic cat had worn off.

The idea of a puma stalking the Surrey countryside caught the imagination of both press and public. A puma was not believed to be dangerous to anything other than farm stock so there was no fear for public safety and therefore no panic. Yet, in spite of the belief that they were hunting a tame animal, neither police nor civilian searchers found a big cat to end the speculation, and over the years tantalising reports of brief sightings continued to trickle into the media headlines.

In 1972, Dennis Long of Fleet was one of a number of witnesses who saw a big cat outside Fleet Station not far from Bushylease Farm. Railway-worker Vic Carr confirmed the sighting, but whatever it was they saw, it did not appear to be a puma, nor did it match any of the animals seen by Edward Blanks and his family. The Fleet Station cat reported by the witnesses was described as having a black head and a brown body, with grey markings – just to add to the confusion.

The police frequently dismissed such conflicting descriptions by members of the public as mass hysteria or mistaken identity, though it is difficult to understand why PC Anthony Thomas and his colleague were unable to identify the animal they encountered in the Queen Elizabeth Park, Farnborough, in June of that year. PC Thomas said, 'It was in the early hours of the morning but the light was good. It stood about ten yards away from me. It was three or four times the size of a cat, with a long tail and pointed ears. It was definitely not a dog or a fox. But I'm not saying it was definitely a puma.'

A puma is an easily recognisable cat, so it is strange that a policeman, trained to be observant, could not positively identify the animal he saw at such close quarters. But PC Thomas was not alone in his reticence to name the species of the feline he had encountered. This is surprising when one considers that there are only a few big cat species existing in modern times and they are each distinctive in appearance.

In fact just nine feline species survive that could be described as big cats; all others, such as the cave lion, the true and false sabretooths, have existed worldwide but are now extinct, possibly due to the emergence of man as a species. The largest of all the surviving great cats is the tiger, very distinctive in shape and coat pattern, its bold dark stripes on the golden pelage varying only in the density of the background colour. No melanistic (black) tigers have ever been recorded.

The second largest cat is the lion, the female of which could very easily match the description given of some animals seen roaming the British countryside, but the lion is a mainly ground-living species, relying on its size and power more than secrecy and stealth for its hunting and protection. Certainly numerous lions are kept in wildlife parks and zoos, for they adapt to captivity easily and breed successfully in captive conditions, and some could have escaped or been released into the British countryside. The lion's behaviour makes it highly unlikely that it could continue to elude searchers for long. Any lion known to have escaped would generally have been recovered within hours rather than days, partly due to the fact that, having no natural predators other than man, the lion does not instinctively seek cover but will settle quite happily on open ground. A lioness would certainly match some of the eye-witness descriptions of a large and sleek fawn or golden brown cat, but it seems improbable that a large number of such cats could continue to exist wild in Britain without at least some being caught.

The South American jaguar is smaller than a lion, though it is still a big, powerful and very dangerous cat. Its normal coat colour is gold with black rosettes but the species does also produce a black form. However, melanistic jaguars are uncommon compared to the spotted kind. In its natural environment the jaguar preys on monkeys, and so one could expect human casualties if a number of jaguars were loose in the British Isles.

The leopard's coat pattern is very similar to that of the jaguar, except that its rosettes lack the central dot of the bigger New World cat. It frequently throws a melanistic form and also preys on monkeys. It is the commonest of all the big cats, with a vast and varied territory.

The cheetah is also spotted but its long legs and lanky shape make it easily distinguished from the leopard. It is rarely known to throw a melanistic form.

The puma, also called the North American cougar or mountain-lion, is a smaller, less powerful cat than the other large species. It is a plain brown cat in varying shades from reddish to pale fawn, similar to the lioness. Its natural prey consists of rabbits, hares and small deer. A black form has never been known in captivity.

Also in the medium range of the larger cats are the clouded leopard and the snow leopard, both with distinctive coat patterns of diffused and blotched spots on pale creamy-fawn or gold backgrounds. They are quite rare cats with very specialised lifestyles.

The last cat that could really be included in the big cat list is the lynx. Though of only medium size and rather indistinct coat pattern, this cat is easily recognised by its tufted ears and short bobbed tail.

The only known feline species indigenous to the British Isles in historic times is *Felis silvestris silvestris*, commonly called the Scottish wildcat. Because of its rarity, most people are unfamiliar with it and it has been confused with sightings of panther-size cats around the countryside. The wildcat, however, is not much larger than a domestic cat and, in spite of its ferocity, cannot be classed as a big cat.

With so many people claiming clear sightings of big cats across Britain, and with such a short list of possible cats to choose from, it is hard to understand why witnesses are so confused about the species they have seen.

Certainly there have been escapees from wildlife parks, zoos and private collections, but most of those recorded have turned up within hours or days of being listed as missing. Even cats whose lifestyle would make discovery extremely difficult have finally lost their bid for freedom. Possibly the most notable of these was the clouded leopard that escaped from John Aspinal's wildlife park and remained at liberty for about six months before finally being shot by a farmer.

In 1980, following a number of big cat sightings in the area around Cannich in Inverness-shire, farmer Ted Noble set a trap on the hillside below the house of Miss Jessie Chisholm who lived in an isolated situation, surrounded by forestry, and who constantly reported seeing big cats in the region of her garden. The trap was quite small and flimsy, being made of wood and wire, but on the 29th October it was found to have caught an adult female puma. It was taken to the Highland Wildlife Park at Kincraigh, where it eventually died of natural causes. The animal was quite tame, but its origins remain undiscovered. Although capture of the puma should have vindicated the witnesses claiming to have seen big cats in the area, it actually confused the situation for witnesses stated that the cat which was trapped was not the same as the cats they had seen – a fact emphasised in the description by a scientific officer from the Institute of Terrestrial Ecology who claimed to have seen a jet-black cat the size of an Alsatian on a sunny morning in the forest behind Miss Chisholm's house.

In the summer of the following year, police in East Berkshire were staked out in the grounds of the public school, Wellington College, attempting to capture a reported puma that had been sighted in the grounds and surrounding woodland. The fact that the Scottish puma had been captured by a hill farmer in a home-made wooden trap should have given the Berkshire police hope, but they were hampered by not knowing what they were actually hunting as witnesses had reported brown, fawn and jet-black animals in the area.

In the same month as the South Molton farmer, Eric Ley, was requesting police assistance to help protect his diminishing flocks – April 1983 – other armed police officers with a helicopter were hunting a strange big catlike animal reported near the village of Stokenchurch in Buckinghamshire. It was identified by the police as a puma, witnesses describing the animal as a feline the size of an Alsatian, slender with a long thick tail, a small head and short legs. Its colour was a deep fawn with merging black spots. The animal was watched for about half an hour by witnesses, one of whom, Mr Viccars, said, 'None of us is in any doubt that it was a puma.'

Such conviction was odd, considering the clearly described

colour of the animal. Pumas are fawn, and only spotted as young cubs. Either it was a young puma and not the size of an Alsatian dog, or it was not spotted, or it was not a puma!

It was in an atmosphere of similar confusion that the police officers, farmers and Royal Marine Commandos found themselves in North Devon in 1983. If all witnesses were claiming to see a similar animal, and it was a cat they were hunting, the species should have been easy to identify from so few possibilities. The trouble was that witnesses were describing creatures of different sizes and different colours, some identified as cats, others as dogs, or of inconclusive form.

Obviously some descriptions could be discarded as the result of tricks of light, of mistaken identity or even general ignorance. Even with clear daylight sightings of reasonable duration by sensible, honest and sincere witnesses, the descriptions of the animals seen seldom matched exactly, in anything but size, any of the nine known species of big cats.

The most popular comparison was with a black panther, the animal described as the size of a Labrador or Alsatian dog, weighing between 70lbs and 120lbs, with a broad flat catlike head, small upright ears similar to those of a household cat, and with a long sweeping tail that curled up at the end. Some witnesses insisted that the animals they had seen had a white blaze on the chest or white feet, or were coloured dark or light-grey, brown or even cream, sometimes with darker heads, or with bands down the back.

It was little wonder that zoologists denied that the descriptions could be of large cats, and the police, accepting the expert's advice, believed that a number of the sightings were of roaming dogs, not cats, terrorising the North Devon countryside.

The marines felt confident that they were more than a match for any dog that was preying on the local flocks around South Molton. For their part, the police were relieved that the professionals had been called in to control a situation that was rapidly getting out of hand. Farmers hoped that – dog or cat – whatever it was that was attacking their flocks had its days numbered. The media hovered, fascinated by the whole affair, eager to see the mystery finally solved.

With the hunt for the beast of Exmoor in expert hands and so much force gathered against it, clearly the beast, or beasts, had no chance of survival. Just two questions remained to be answered: what was it, and when would it be killed?

4

The End of Operation Beastie

Having assessed the situation and decided that the inclement weather would deter most amateur beast hunters, Sergeant Major Andy Wilkins and his men moved quietly back to the cattle shed at Drewstone Farm and set up camp again. The farmers assisted them to close up the area, knowing that a repeat of the circus would result in the marines being recalled to Lympstone and the last chance of defeating the beast would be gone. Even the media seemed to sense that they had gone too far. Individual reporters actually staying in the area understood what the farmers were facing, having seen for themselves the difficult terrain involved in the search and the carnage resulting from the beast's attacks.

The police were only too happy to hand the problem back to the marines. Sergeant Goodman of South Molton police said later, 'It was a situation we were not experienced or trained for. We were used to looking for people, not animals. We just didn't know where to begin, yet something had to be done about the predator, whatever it was.'

Despite the relief of the farmers and police officers, there remained an element of disquiet. Andy Wilkins said later, 'I don't think the civilians understood what we were. They seemed to think we were dangerous and that no woman or child was safe with us around. They needed us, but they were afraid of us. It was a very strange situation.'

Whatever the difficulties, the marines once more set about their task with the same dedication as they would approach a battle objective. Gradually they built up a pretty good picture of the creature they were hunting. Andy Wilkins said, 'The animal was big, Great Dane size, standing at least knee-high, maybe a couple of inches above on someone my size. (He is about six foot three in height.) It was long-bodied with thick-set powerful shoulders, almost no neck and a squat ugly quite small round head with pricked ears. It was dark brown or black. Some reports described white markings, a white chest spot and white socks, but we suspected that this could be the result of drying clay splattered on the animal. The weather was very wet and the ground in the area was heavy clay. If the animal had been wading through the stuff, it was heavy enough for its feet to sink into the clay, giving it the effect of lighter coloured legs and possibly a pale clay splattered chest. We also considered that the colour variation could be due to a wet or dry coat, the animal being dark brown but appearing black when seen wet.'

Certainly it was possible to explain some of the differences in the witnesses' descriptions in this way, but not the tracks. The Sergeant Major found tracks that suggested there was, in fact, more than one beast.

'I could easily recognise one animal by its tracks as it had a deformed paw and limped,' he said. 'One claw and toe on its front foot appeared to have been ripped off and I felt it might have had its foot caught in a snare at some time. This was the big one, but I also tracked a second animal with a much smaller foot, apparently running with it at one time. The size of the smaller animal matched the description given by some witnesses that there was a second smaller cat being seen in the area, though whether this meant the big one had young or was simply running with a smaller cat we had no way of knowing. The smaller cat would have been about the size of a springer spaniel.'

The marines hoped to be able to bait the animal to within range of their guns, in a situation where they could fire. As they had discovered so quickly on their first attempt, when John had seen the creature but been unable to fire because of the proximity of a farmhouse, not only did they have to get the animal within range, they also had to get it into a suitable target position.

They decided to operate along the old disused railway line where John had seen the animal and where it had constantly been tracked. That appeared to be their best chance of ambushing the beast for it seemed to use the line frequently as a route during its night hunting. For the first couple of nights the marines were deployed in sniper positions in hides, with a dead bullock staked out as bait, but with no result. A local builder offered to provide scaffold to build observation towers, and these were constructed along the route, giving the snipers a much wider vision, at the same time keeping them out of sight and even reach of the animal they hunted. Although there had been no evidence that the beast would attack man, the size and power of the creature was frightening and no one knew how it would react when fired upon. Certainly there have been reports of lions and tigers continuing their attack on hunters after receiving a mortal wound. Not even the highly trained Marine Commandos fancied being on the receiving end of an attack by the beast of Exmoor.

Given all the equipment and the manpower provided by the marines, there were still problems. One was the lack of night sights. Although the snipers worked in pairs, they had only one image intensifier between them, and this meant that only one sniper could see and target the animal if it appeared. The lack of equipment was a direct result of the war in the Falklands, where the marines had distinguished themselves in battle but where so much equipment had been destroyed or damaged. In 1983 not all the lost equipment had been replaced.

After finding that a bullock as bait proved to be no enticement to the beast, the marines tried another tack. They obtained a live but sickly lamb from one of the farms and tied lumps of poisoned liver, wrapped in wool, around the animal's neck before tethering it out in the area of the route known to be used by the beast. The results were strange, if unsuccessful. The following morning the marines found the lamb alive, with no wounds, yet the bait had been torn from its neck and had vanished. When I suggested that birds could have carried off the bait, Andy was unconvinced.

He told me, 'We really tied it on tightly with strong cord. It would have taken some strength to get it off and carry away the meat. Not even a bird of prey could have done it so neatly.'

It was possible that a small predator with sharp teeth could have gnawed through the cord and carried off the pieces of liver without hurting the lamb, but like so many incidents that occurred during the hunt for the mystery beast, the incident has never been satisfactorily explained. My own theory is that a small mammal, such as a stoat or a weasel, a mink or even a rat may have been the mystery thief. A creature too small to tackle the lamb, but attracted by the scent of the meat, could have leapt up unseen by the watchers looking for an animal the size of a Great Dane and snatched away at the inviting chunks of offal until the cord was bitten through and the deadly treat retrieved.

Be that as it may, whatever was attracted by the free if ultimately costly meal, it was not the Exmoor beast, which continued to choose its own dinner from the surrounding grazing sheep.

The marines might have been short of equipment but they certainly were not short of advice. Numerous people contacted the police with ideas, and calls were also received at the

Royal Marine Training Centre at Lympstone, where they were recorded. Among the more outlandish suggestions was one from a man claiming to have been a member of the Special Forces and also to have seen the beast. He described it as looking like a llama, with a head that could turn sixty degrees and eyes like spotlights. Another caller suggested that the beast was a pig, and yet another that it was a being from another planet, the man claiming to have sighted the flying saucer. One person living on Exmoor claimed to have proof that the beast was in fact a member of a local family who was affected at certain times, changing into a werewolf and escaping from his family's custody to attack sheep on the moor.

Andy Wilkins recalls a medium who was brought to Eric Ley's farmhouse and dangled a gold watch over a map of the area, claiming she could predict the beast's movements. He told me wryly that 'everywhere she sent us the beast actually appeared in the opposite direction'.

Numerous white hunters appeared, some genuine, with experience of living and hunting in places such as Africa and Malaya; others were idiots with Rambo aspirations and no knowledge of trapping anything larger than a mouse.

Some arrived on their own, others were sent, complete with reporters and film crews, sponsored by various members of the media. One man with a sound reputation was Eddie Magee who had gained fame by assisting the police in the manhunt for the killer Barry Purdom. The marines were neither impressed by his knowledge nor his actions. He arrived complete with a film crew and the boast that, if it were there, he would get it! The marines were mystified when he returned each morning, bright-eyed and bone-dry after a night's supposed hunting, while they were soaking wet and exhausted. The mystery was explained by the famous tracker spending his nights tucked up warmly in his hotel bed. An understandable action to take in the pouring rain, but not one calculated to endear him to the wet and weary marines. Like most other such visitors to the scene, Mr Magee soon retreated to warmer and easier climes away from the cold rain-lashed Exmoor landscape.

Another man appeared claiming to be part Red Indian, part gypsy. Calling himself the Tracker, he suggested that the mystery predator was some sort of Moon Beast. He also claimed to have helped the police in Wales by hunting some wolves that had escaped from a wildlife park. Although the police in Wales agreed he had been present during the wolf hunt, they were more than a little reluctant to suggest he had assisted them.

One man turned up with an Alsatian dog that he claimed could track anything down and kill it. The Sergeant Major pointed out that the creature they were hunting was about three times the size of the dog and, for the dog's safety, sent him on his way.

Some offers of help were received with thanks by the marines, including those of a local gamekeeper. One Exmoor farmer phoned the marine camp wanting landmines laid on the moor because, he claimed, the beast was killing on his land. The marines went up to have a look round his farm but said they could not lay landmines in the area, pointing out tactfully that the mines would account for more sheep and local walkers than unidentified beasts.

By this time the predator, obviously aware of the hunters, had widened its hunting territory. If they had not actually seen it, most of the hunters had now heard the scream of the beast.

Andy Wilkins said, 'It was heard a lot. I sat in a chicken-house one night in the middle of the third week with another bloke and we heard it scream again as it followed the line of the old railway line. It always seemed to scream after it had killed rather than before, as if it was announcing the fact. The area it covered was getting bigger and we were no further on to establishing a pattern to its behaviour.'

Dog or cat? The police and marines were still confused,

1   Farmer Eric Ley (right) with an armed patrol setting out in April 1983 to hunt down the beast of Exmoor. (Photo: Tony Freeman)

2   A detachment of Royal Marines Commandos, led by Sergeant Major Wilkins, was called in to dispose of the killer. (Photo: Devon News Agency)

3 Police Sergeant Dave Goodman and PC Martin Abbot at South Molton police station in 1992.

4 Andy Wilkins, ex-Royal Marines Commandos, on Dartmoor in 1992 believes there is more than one big cat still at large in the Devon countryside.

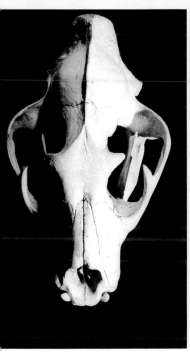
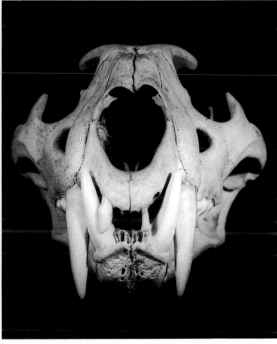

5–6 Mystery skull found on Dartmoor, measuring more than 270mm in length and showing striking dentition. (Photos: Andrew Barker)

7 Plaster cast of footprint left by Tonmawr cat (left) compared with that of a leopard.

8, 9, 10 Two photographs, taken by the author, of a big black cat on a Welsh hillside near Tonmawr. Seven years later she returned to the hillside and removed the arched branch seen in the picture on the right and indicating the cat's size.

some convinced it was one, some equally sure it was the other. The supporters of the rogue dog theory seemed to have turned up evidence when a man from Woodbury phoned to say he had sold a dog to a man in Barnstaple, a Doberman crossed with a Rottweiler, that killed prey by breaking the neck and often eating the ears, a trait in evidence at a number of the beast kills. Andy Wilkins was convinced they had found the identity of the beast at last. When the buyer was traced, the dog was found to be dead, so they had to go back to square one.

Another lead from Barnstaple appeared to support the cat theory. This was the story of a butcher who had kept a puma as a guard 'dog'. It was said that the animal had frequently escaped and was constantly found wandering about the town and taken to the local police station. The butcher had left the country and, despite a concentrated search, the police were unable to trace his whereabouts. Later, while making a half-hour programme about mystery cats in Britain, the BBC television 'Tomorrow's World' team claimed to have traced the butcher and to have interviewed the vet who had put the puma down when it was dying of old age.

Whether the butcher's puma was dead or alive, it was not a contender for the identity of the beast unless the majority of witnesses who had claimed sightings were completely wrong about the colour of the animal they had seen, for the beast was usually described as black or a very dark brown or grey and pumas are fawn or golden brown.

As the weeks passed, the marines grew weary. Andy Wilkins recalls, 'The kills continued about every four or five days, sometimes two days, over a wide area and we worked out a system with the local farmers whereby we could call them in and cordon off an area so that we could sweep through. Then, if it was seen and we were almost certain from the description that it was the beast, we would move in. It was seen by a farmer's wife on horseback at a place called Hill Town Farm, and she described it accurately, so we got out there quickly, the posse of farmers joining us. We managed to cordon off the area and beat the woods, but it evaded us.' He added ruefully, 'In fact, I fell into a slurry pit and got my leg trapped, which everyone found very amusing. They didn't have any trousers to fit me and I ended the day partly-clad which undoubtedly provided a lot of laughter for the locals down at the pub.'

His judgement had been correct – about amusing the locals – but even he failed to appreciate the impact of the tale. Nine years later I visited the farm and met the farmer, Melvin Nichols, and one of the first stories he told me was of Andy and the slurry pit.

Up to this time the Sergeant Major had heard the frightening scream of the beast and had found its tracks, and these had given him some indication of its weight and size, but he had not actually seen the creature for himself. At the beginning of the fourth week, while Andy was being driven by a local woman, Mrs Lynn Lock, to the area of a beast sighting, they suddenly saw the animal bounding across a field.

'It was mid-afternoon,' he said, 'when we spotted a large black animal quartering and sniffing across a field approximately four hundred yards from us. It definitely wasn't a dog, but I can't honestly say exactly what it was. It was big and powerful, about the size of a mastiff. It moved quite quickly and disappeared into a patch of woodland alongside a stream. It was the first time I'd actually seen the beast, and it was in daylight. By this time the area it covered was spreading from South Molton to North Molton and up towards Exmoor itself, so we were starting to move with the sightings. We got a local trapper in from the Tavistock area, and he was the only guy to say that we wouldn't catch it in five minutes.'

Despite the cat advocates now outnumbering the dog theorists, it was decided to make one last attempt to attract a rogue dog, as the official line to the public was still that they were hunting a feral dog. The police even paraded a selection of dogs for a press call, suggesting that the beast of Exmoor was a combination of the breeds mastiff and lurcher. At the trapper's suggestion a couple of bitches in season were walked for miles across the countryside, hoping to lure the suggested dog by the scent. The result was disappointing for those still clinging to the dog theory. As one marine stated wearily, 'We covered twenty miles in all. In the end the bitches were knackered and we had to carry them home!'

It was possibly the last attempt to prove that the beast was of canine descent, and its lack of success gave those in favour of a feline almost total control. If the predator was a rogue dog, it was behaving in a very undog-like manner by failing to respond to any canine enticements.

The marines were beginning to feel the strain and the lack of sleep. To give them a break some men from 42 Commando were sent to relieve them. The local trapper was with one of the newly arrived marine snipers when suddenly they saw the animal. The sniper didn't fire because he felt that the target was too far away. When later they paced out the distance, the Sergeant Major was frustrated to discover that the creature had been only 500 metres away and thus within range.

Soon the Sergeant Major had even more reason to feel annoyed, with the arrival of the relief marines. The original group of men had seen the carnage and the distress caused among the farming community and they took seriously their task to eliminate the predator. Understandably the relief men lacked both the dedication and the sense of responsibility, treating the whole hunt as a bit of fun and a break from barracks routine. After all, unlike many of the situations in which the marines could find themselves, the beast was not going to shoot back, or first.

One pair of relief commandos – no doubt thinking they were stuck up a tower for no real purpose, possibly only looking for a roaming dog – became bored and decided to play hookie. Quietly they climbed down from their perch on an observation platform and sneaked off to the local pub for a pint. They returned to discover that the beast had taken advantage of their absence and had killed within fifty metres of their hide.

It was some time before the story filtered back to the Sergeant Major who was furious. The men were returned to barracks and the original team returned to the field.

The beast appeared to enjoy a charmed life. On the few occasions it had been within range of the sniper's guns, it had always escaped because of the circumstances of the sighting. Although the hunters were only too aware that their quarry was a flesh and blood creature, yet many sensible men grew in awe of it, as if the beast had superhuman powers or extraordinary intelligence.

One of the marines told me, 'It was almost as if it was playing with us, showing itself only when it knew we couldn't fire, just to tease us. It even seemed to know what we were going to do before we did ourselves. It seemed to challenge us.'

Whether it was highly intelligent or just very lucky, the beast certainly knew it was being hunted and acted accordingly. It would use cover to move around, often adding miles to its route to evade being seen, skirting round fields, keeping to the shelter of the hedgerows rather than crossing open land. None the less, its caution did not affect its appetite for Devon lamb and the kills continued to multiply, averaging two a week and sometimes more. If it ever actually had a pattern to its movements, the knowledge of hunters after it clearly changed its instinctive behaviour.

In an attempt to keep it within range, the marines shifted the centre of operations and the hides up towards North Molton, and this caused problems. It was now necessary to ferry the men around the countryside for they were no longer positioned within walking distance of the camp.

With the hunt in its fifth week, local opinion began to turn against the presence of the marines. It seemed to residents that the return of the marines should have ended the whole sorry business. Their lack of success, the failure of their expertise and weaponry against an animal led to disappointment and frustration which was expressed locally in a bitterness that could still be sensed nine years later.

It did not help local acceptance that, although the marines were highly trained in warfare techniques and jungle or desert survival, many of these city lads knew nothing of ordinary everyday life in a farming and country community. This was illustrated when, during a helicopter sweep of the countryside, one of the marines spotted the telltale form of a downed sheep. Thinking the animal might have been a victim of the beast, they landed to check it out. The sheep, a ewe, was still alive but bleeding from the head. The marine, taking pity on the poor creature, ended its misery with a bullet. Unfortunately the whole episode was watched from across the fields, by a local farmer. Far from being injured, the ewe had simply rolled on her back and needed a firm haul on her fleece to get her back on her feet. The blood had been the result of birds pecking near her eyes. Any farmer would have recognised the situation at once. The luckless marine, unfamiliar with sheep except when served with mint sauce, had killed a healthy animal out of mistaken compassion.

The outraged owner was informed by the farmer who had witnessed the incident and a letter demanding £200 in compensation was swiftly on its way to the marine commander.

The marines also shot a number of dogs that were spotted in the act of attacking sheep, but irate and bereaved owners would not, or could not, believe that their pets had been involved in sheep worrying and accusations were made of a 'shoot anything that moves' campaign. One worried pet-owner is reputed to have painted the word DOG in large white letters on his black Labrador in an attempt to protect it from being mistaken for the now accepted feline beast and shot.

At last, however, the marines got the chance to shoot at something other than fallen sheep or pet dogs.

John, the first marine to have seen the beast, was in a hide with a marine called Ginge, when Ginge, using the night sight, spotted the creature coming towards them and was able to take aim and fire. Immediately the night sight whitened out with the glare, destroying his vision, as the beast came rushing up the gully towards the startled marines. Blindly Ginge fired two more shots and the beast made off at tremendous speed over the hill and out of sight, leaving the two shaken marines uncertain as to whether they had succeeded in hitting the target.

The following day the marines performed a reconstruction, estimating that the beast should have been hit in the lower abdomen, just in front of its hind legs, if it was hit at all. Unfortunately the beast's luck had held once more. Ginge had picked up John's rifle instead of his own, so it had not been zeroed in to his sight, which meant he could have misaimed by a fraction. During a concentrated search of the area no blood was discovered, suggesting that the beast had again escaped unscathed from its hunters.

What had amazed and slightly worried the marines was the beast's behaviour after the first shot. Instead of retreating from the line of fire, it had appeared to go into the attack, only the subsequent firing finally scaring it off.

They never had another chance to shoot the beast again. As if the animal itself had been unnerved by the encounter, it once more shifted its territory. At the end of the sixth week the marines were on the move up on to Exmoor itself, but none of them ever had the beast in their rifle sights again.

People were jumping at shadows, every wandering domestic cat or unaccompanied dog was being accused of resembling the beast. Calls were being received by the marines and the police claiming sightings of the beast miles apart at the same time. After seventy-eight days in the rough, weary and defeated by an unknown opponent, the marines pulled out.

The beast was triumphant.

Andy Wilkins said years later: 'It was a very strange

experience. The beast seemed to bring out the best and the worst in people. It also produced a number of cranks and nutters, and yet a number of friendships were formed during the back-breaking sleepless days and nights on the moors, friendships that have remained over the years. We were pulled out on Thursday, 23rd July 1983, and on the Friday I walked out of the camp at Lympstone as a civilian.'

Operation Beastie had lasted 78 days.

After he had left the marines Andy Wilkins, like so many others involved in the hunt, didn't entirely give up the search. It was like a personal challenge, to bring the mystery predator finally to book. In his spare time he spent the following years wandering the moors, his civilian gun at the ready, his finger on the trigger, waiting for the moment when he would come face to face with his elusive adversary.

He added, 'When I look back I honestly believe that hunting the beast helped to break up my marriage and changed my life completely. Nothing has ever been the same for me since I went up to South Molton and yet, for all the time and manpower spent, we still don't really know what we were up against. And it's still there, still killing on the same farms. What I do know is that it's not a dog, and there's more than one of them, whatever they are.'

5

Police Detection

If the marines could go back to barracks and attempt to put Operation Beastie behind them, returning to more normal situations such as the world battlefields and the uncertain hospitality of Northern Ireland, the Exmoor police had no such opportunities. Like the unfortunate farmers, they lived and worked in beast country and, with the marines gone, the residents once more turned to the police for help in combating the predator that continued to decimate their flocks. The police were sympathetic, and helpless. If the élite commandos had failed, how could a policeman – more used to pounding pavements than beating through bushes – succeed?

Police Sergeant Dave Goodman first became involved when Eric Ley requested information concerning his rights to shoot a dog that appeared to be preying on his lambs. In a rural area where most of the farms were hill farms and most stock was hill sheep, incidents of dogs worrying were not uncommon. After young Susan Fernandez reported her sighting of a large black cat, the rumours began. As the kills increased, Eric Ley returned to the police station to press for the use of a police helicopter and a pack of hounds.

At first the police believed that only Drewstone Farm was losing sheep to the mystery predator. Once the press got hold of the story, they were amazed by the number of kills being reported. The kills were unusual for the ferocity of the attacks and the amount of meat stripped from the carcases in a matter of hours.

'We always do get a number of sheep killed by dogs,' said Sergeant Goodman, 'but these kills stood out as being different from the usual dog attacks. The beast always seemed to start on the head, it then ate down the neck, taking out a lot of the meat around the ribs, very often taking all the innards, but leaving the ribs intact. Someone said that it was more catlike than doglike behaviour because, if it was a dog, it would have chewed up the bones.'

Years later, in the once more peaceful police station in South Molton, Dave Goodman now has time to reflect on the events of 1983. He accepts that what happened at South Molton was not unique. The pattern of sheep kills and cat sightings have occurred in other parts of the country, even other parts of Devon. He told me he didn't know why South Molton received so much attention from the media. 'I suppose it was the presence of Andy and the marines that made the difference, made our beast so much more news-worthy than other similar situations. The force in Surrey sent us some stuff about what had happened there, and we had offers of help from all over the country, some of it from people just out to make themselves a bob or two. Others were genuine and really wanted to help.'

When the marines pulled out, the police were suddenly left facing the problem alone again, with perhaps a little more knowledge than before but still no nearer knowing what species of animal they were hunting.

'It was a strange thing,' added Sergeant Goodman. 'I interviewed a number of people that I had no doubt had actually seen the beast, often quite clearly and in good light, but no one could actually identify the species of animal they had seen. When we asked them "What was it?" they would say "I don't know" – even though they would have seen the different cats on the telly and in zoos and books for comparison. They could describe it vividly but they hadn't got a clue what it was. They'd say it was a bit like a puma, or the nearest thing to it is a panther, but none of them would ever exactly identify the animal.'

One theory suggested to the police to explain this was that the beast was not one species but a sort of hybrid of two. Sergeant Goodman said, 'We also believed there was more than one because some very sincere and honest witnesses were describing different coloured animals. One was a pure black with a shiny coat, one a dark grey, but there were also other colours, even a sort of mottled coat.'

In retrospect, the police accept that they made mistakes because they were dealing with a situation for which they were neither trained nor prepared. Although there was a great deal of evidence to suggest that other areas were facing, or had faced, the same problem, including big cats being seen in other parts of Devon, the South Molton officers never requested information from the different police stations involved. It is difficult to understand why no attempt was made to see if sightings elsewhere could be linked to the Exmoor beast. After all, if the beast was one of the known big cat species, then it could easily have had a hunting territory covering the whole of Devon, moving from one killing ground to another to avoid detection. That could also have explained where the beast had come from. Even if no one had reported losing a big cat in Devon, someone might have lost one elsewhere. it could easily have made its way to the wild and wooded moorlands from some other part of the British Isles. Liaising with other areas and mapping out times and places of earlier sightings could have revealed the movements of one animal across the country from its original home. Yet, simple as it may seem, this was never attempted.

Neither was a professional zoologist contacted, in an

attempt to work out which species they were hunting or to predict the creature's movements from a study of feline behaviour. In fact the full extent of research into big cats by the South Molton police was reference to the few wildlife books kept at the station.

When I asked Sergeant Goodman why – despite the huge expense, the enormous manpower and the sophisticated technology ranged against it – the beast had not been caught or killed, he shrugged. 'You mean, why did we fail? It's difficult to say. There wasn't that much money put into the hunt, and there were only a few marines. It would work out at about two marines per twenty square miles and, with possibly two cats, the animals could keep well clear of the marines. This was proved, wasn't it? Until the marines went in, it appeared to be killing just on Drewstone Farm, or very close to Drewstone, but within two or three days of the marines going in, it was killing at East Ansty and Bray Ford, I mean, it must be a crafty thing that knows it's being hunted. So to put twelve marines into one hundred square miles, to catch one animal, the chances are on the side of the beast, aren't they? It is going to be more cautious, and faster than a human being.'

Other police forces across the whole of the British Isles have felt the same frustration, yet to date no attempt has been made anywhere to pool their slowly acquired knowledge. The Surrey police contacted their South Molton colleagues, with a view to offering what advice and assistance they could, but even then it would seem to have been a rather half-hearted affair – unless, of course, the South Molton police had simply ignored their advice. Certainly the Exmoor beast hunt of the 1980s seems to have added little more to our knowledge of how to deal with a large predator loose in the British countryside than the Surrey puma hunt twenty years earlier. That is not due to any lack of interest on the part of individual officers involved in the various hunts. Martin Abbot was one of the first police officers at South Molton to accept the possibility that the rogue dog was in fact a feral big cat, despite the tide of opinion running against him. Years later, when I met him again, the situation was very different: now no one even suggested the beast was anything but feline. The only question was, of what species?

As Sergeant Goodman said to me in 1992, 'The beast was definitely not a dog. I have a hell of a lot of respect for it. I would like to know what it is, but I don't know that I'd like to see it shot and strung up. It gave us a lot of hard work at the time, but it was very enjoyable in a way. After all, I must be one of the few policemen in the country that has had to deal with something like this.' He paused, and then added quietly, 'I really would like to know what it is before I retire.'

The South Molton police do still receive reports of sightings of the beast but they number no more than a few a year now. At the same time, Dave Goodman and Martin Abbot know that even a trickle indicates that the beast is still there, hunting through the woods and fields around their small market-town, and that any week, any day, the whole circus could begin again.

The beast or its relatives have not moved on; it is only that the people who live in or around the beast's territory no longer bother to report sightings or their slaughtered stock. The high hopes of May 1983 have been deflated to a dismal acceptance of the situation. The beast exists. Nothing tried by man has succeeded in doing more than widen its territory and teach it caution.

Yet if the old hands have grown tired of the game and given up to the superiority of the beast, there is a generation of new hunters only too willing to take their places.

Like others, one of these new hunters, Detective Steve Ashcroft of the Metropolitan Regional Crime Squad, was at school when the unidentified Exmoor beast first caught his imagination. Later he began to spend his free time researching the mystery with the same dedication and skill as he brought to his work as a police detective. Like so many beast hunters, he took it as a personal challenge to solve the mystery with a perfectly logical explanation.

'As far as I can see,' he says, 'no one has yet looked at the problem in the same way as one would study the evidence of a crime, and that's what I intend to do. Taking all the evidence, I'll use a process of elimination to sort out the facts from the fiction.'

With a view to collecting all the facts, Detective Ashcroft publicly invited all the witnesses that had seen mystery felines around the British countryside to contact him. He also wanted all those who had been hunting the various beasts to get in touch so that they could pool their knowledge, discuss the evidence and co-ordinate it. His task was not made easy by the lack of record-keeping.

He looked first at the number of big cats owned and licenced throughout Britain since the passing of the 1976 Dangerous Wild Animals Act, which required all such exotic pets to be recorded. 'It's just a nightmare,' he told me. 'You see a zoo listed as having seven big cats and phone them, to be told they have only three, and have no idea of the where-abouts of the missing four. It's not that they are admitting to losing them. The present staff just don't know anything about any other big cats. And it's worse when trying to trace private collections.'

It is hardly surprising that the licencing of such animals is in a state of total confusion. 'Two registered cats can become six in a year with the successful rearing of one litter of cubs. Equally, two can die of natural causes within the same time span, leaving that particular zoo, or owner, with no big cats. And in the present economic climate, with the rising cost of feeding and veterinary care, together with the change in public attitude towards animals in cages and the declining popularity of zoos, it is more than likely that dead big cats will not be replaced.'

In one case in 1992, Detective Ashcroft received reports of a puma being sighted by a number of very reliable witnesses in an area of woodland. He contacted the local zoo, to be told cheerfully, yes, it was one of theirs. A gale had damaged the puma enclosure, allowing one animal to escape. When he asked what they intended to do about retrieving the puma, he was told, nothing. The cost of a hunt to recapture the beast would have been far greater than the simple act of acquiring a replacement. Pumas are not a danger to the public, so the poor frightened beast was on its own, surviving in the British countryside until either it was shot by a surprised farmer or it starved to death in a hard winter.

Even so, if the police can accept the reality of an occasional lost puma or a mislaid leopard, such animals cannot explain the vast number of sightings of cats that do not exactly resemble those that could have escaped. As Sergeant Goodman noted, witnesses never seem to be able to identify exactly the species of felines they have seen, and the few photographs taken of the mystery cats simply confuse rather than solve the puzzle.

In 1982, exactly a year before Eric Ley went into South Molton police station to complain about a mystery predator killing his lambs, I had managed to photograph a leopard-size black cat at Tonmawr in Wales. (See pages 54–5.) A melanistic leopard perhaps? Except it had a grey cub with dark markings, spots and thin stripes, in the coat. Maybe a trick of light?

A local resident, Steve Joyce, photographed the cub showing its coat pattern quite clearly. (See pages 86–7.) He also photographed a large grey cat with what appeared to be a white or cream chest, seated on the hillside. (See pages 86–7.) No known cats have such coloration. Could this be photographic evidence that witnesses are not mistaken when describing cats that apparently do not exist?

Photographic evidence is not proof of anything other than the use of a camera. Photographs can be distorted, altered, or even employed as part of an elaborate hoax. Like circumstantial evidence in a court case, it is evidence but not conclusive proof.

To know what the Exmoor beast is, one needs it in a cage or on a laboratory table, awaiting dissection.

As the authorities become less prejudiced against the idea of mystery cats roaming the British Isles, so the possibility of capturing one becomes more likely. Although skilled and well-equipped, the marines were looking for the wrong species. By the time they began thinking cat rather than dog, it was too late; the beast knew it was being hunted and took evasive action.

Luck or intelligence? It was impossible to say. It is true, however, that everyone who has ever attempted to track, kill, or capture one of these mystery felines soon comes to respect it, even to admire it.

Police Sergeant Goodman said he wanted to know what it was, but he did not want to see it dead.

Marine Sergeant Major Wilkins said, 'Whatever it was we were hunting, it was highly intelligent. Sometimes it seemed to know what we were doing before we knew ourselves, almost as if it could read our thoughts.'

One Exmoor farmer told me about his personal encounter with the beast. He does not want his name to be known as he is afraid of inviting the anger of his friends and neighbours for failing to end the predator's career when he had the chance to do so. He was shooting on the moors when he suddenly came face to face with the beast, his gun in his hand, his finger on the trigger. Yet he did not fire. Afterwards he said he did not know why, but nothing on earth could have made him pull that trigger. He looked in the golden depths of the animal's eyes and found himself helpless, unable to destroy the beast.

Compassion, or subjected to hypnotic suggestion?

Only time may reveal the truth.

6

Mad Dogs and Englishmen

Once the professionals had been defeated, others felt that now was their chance to tackle the beast. Amateur hunters, aged from ten to eighty, across the whole of the British Isles became convinced that they alone could capture or kill the beast and complete the task that highly skilled and trained combat troops had failed to finish.

Of course most of the enthusiasts only discussed ideas and made suggestions, but some, especially those living in the beast's territory, decided to put their ideas into action. Bait was a constant source of controversy. Surely there was something that the beast would find irresistible, something that could lure it to within the range of an ambitious shot or an amateurishly constructed cage. One man had very definite ideas on how to attract the beast – if it was a cat. Arthur Cademan MBE, who lived in Inverness-shire, not far from Cannich where a puma had been caught, was sure he had the answer.

'Kippers!' he informed me seriously when I was visiting Cannich. 'No cat can resist them. You put kippers in a trap and the beast, if it's a cat, will go in. Kippers!'

I don't know if anyone in the Exmoor area tried kippers, but if not, it must be one of the few more eccentric ideas that hasn't been used to tempt the beast away from its diet of Devon lamb.

The difficulty of enticing the creature into a chosen area with bait is the abundance of natural food to be found in the British countryside. In addition, the beast seemed to adopt random movements. If a wild animal always feeds in the same area, it is possible to clear that particular spot of its usual prey and set up an easy meal to attract the hungry target. Unfortunately, as the marines had discovered all too often, the beast did not keep to any pattern for its night's activities but hit different farms repeatedly at different times and intervals. Over such a wide area it would have been impossible to clear the hillsides of sheep. Yet without clearing the thousands of sheep from the moors there was no way the beast was going to be attracted to bait, live or dead.

Such small considerations did not deter the truly dedicated from trying. One retired gentleman claimed he had invented the perfect beast catcher and he wandered happily along the Devon lanes holding a long pole with a noose dangling from the end, convinced that eventually he and the beast would come face to face and the beast would obligingly pop its head into the rope collar for the perfect fit. Another, retired biologist Nigel Brierley, claimed to be only a whisker away from inventing a powerful cat aphrodisiac. He was convinced that a quick spray of odour of catmint around a chosen field and the beast would be hot foot, bright-eyed and bushy-tailed. He announced to the media that he was growing a field of catmint just to attract the beast, for no cat could resist the scent. Other scents included liberal sprays of aniseed and odour of 'in season' puma.

Local naturalist Trevor Beer had told the *Western Morning News* about black cat sightings, declaring that the beast killing sheep on the moor was definitely a dog, or dogs, until the day when he came face to face with a black panther-like beast on Exmoor.

I was crossing a stream when I looked up and saw this head emerging from the bushes in front of me. It was very broad across the top, with small ears and wide-set green-yellow eyes.

The animal ran very fast and with the gait of a greyhound. It was jet black, sleek and smooth, with very long hind legs. I would estimate it weighed between 80 and 120lbs.

It was more like a panther than anything else I have ever seen. All along I have worked on the basis that it was a dog.

Once converted to the cat theory, Trevor Beer combined forces with beast hunter Brierley. In November 1984 they announced that there was not one but two big cats running on the moors. 'We are getting reports of sightings far apart at almost the same time. And while many of the sightings are of a large black panther-like creature, there are quite a lot of reports of a fawn-coloured beast. I believe there is a puma and a panther on the moor.'

Brierley had a letter published in the *North Devon Advertiser*, asking the public for help with their research.

There are two pieces of information about these animals which are known to us and which could help in identification. These are very important in finding a pattern on the habits of the animals. Firstly, calls lasting approximately two seconds and repeated at four second intervals are fairly strong and resonant, ending on an upward trend. The most common times seem to be between 11 p.m. and 3 a.m. Anyone who hears this call, or has heard it in the last couple of months, please let us know.

Secondly, we have records of sightings last year of black catlike animals the size of a large Labrador showing white on various parts of the body, of a large tawny-coloured animal the size of an Alsatian; and of smaller animals about the size of a dogfox with very dark tabby stripes on grey or tawny background.

The letter suggested that they were no longer looking for just two different animals, a puma and a panther. It also underlined the confusion felt by everyone seriously attempting to identify the Exmoor beast from its description.

Other animal experts in the area avoided the controversy by refusing to acknowledge that the problem existed. Just a few days before the publication of Brierley's letter, the *Western Morning News* reported author and naturalist Brian Carter as stating that he had spent the past thirty years tramping over Dartmoor without ever seeing anything resembling a big cat.

> Stories of sightings run riot around springtime during the lambing season. People who start these stories are scare-mongering.
>
> What concerns me is trigger-happy people who might mistake our own predators for this creature. Animals such as otters will become natural targets. If there are big cats living on Dartmoor, why hasn't one ever been knocked down by a car?
>
> If they are as big as people say, they would cause havoc on moorland farms, attacking livestock – particularly during the winter months when food would be scarce.
>
> I haven't heard any reports of farmers being besieged by big cats.

It is hard to believe that Carter could make such a statement in a paper that only eighteen months earlier had carried a photograph of armed farmers hunting the predator that was preying on their livestock. The headline was 'The Black Beast Strikes Once More'. The same paper also reported 'Anger as sheep flocks are again attacked. Call off Beast bounty – MP.'

Printed alongside Mr Carter's statement was an article describing Trevor Beer's account of his sighting of a 'black panther'.

There was clearly dissension between the animal experts. If Brian Carter was dismissing any other theory than his own, regardless of the evidence before him, he was not alone.

In one North Devon newspaper Noel Allen, chairman of the Exmoor Natural History Society, claimed that the beast of Exmoor never existed. He said arrogantly 'I am certain I would have seen some sign of the beast if it existed.' Did he consider that all the dead sheep with their throats ripped out had committed suicide?

Even some of the converted were still in a confused frame of mind. While examining eye-witness statements, claiming sightings of big brown, tabby and black with white markings, Trevor Beer still responded to my own research on the mystery cat sightings with the words: 'I don't believe there is a separate race of black cats running around the countryside. If there is, and they are in North Devon, then I have wasted thirty-five years as a naturalist without ever having seen one.'

In the same month, he asked me privately what type of cat I thought people might have seen when they described a Labrador-dog-size Siamese cat?

Some witnesses commented scathingly on the experts, suggesting that if a few more of them stopped voicing uninformed opinions and spent more time in beast territory then they might be able to make more helpful observations. Certainly Trevor Beer did exactly that and found himself face to face with a big cat, and within months he was admitting that a number of beasts could exist – a brown puma and a lynx as well as the black leopard-like animal he himself had seen, maybe even hybrid combinations of all three species. For a man who had originally poured scorn on the idea that one big cat could be roaming the moors, it was certainly a drastic change of heart. He wrote a book describing his experience of meeting a beast and led tours across beast country.

Even more outlandish theories began to circulate. The *Daily Express*, having failed to acquire a photograph of the beast despite its bounty offer, reported in 1985 that 20lb of tripe had been stolen from the Minehead farm of Mrs Brenda Cornish by an animal leaving a paw print identified by

experts as that of a wolverene. As with most such identifica-
tions, the 'experts' involved remained anonymous.

Leopard, puma, lynx, dog or wolverene, the beast not only
continued to prey on farmstock and confuse the experts, it
also appeared to be breeding. In the same year as Mrs Cornish
was sitting by her tripe shed with a loaded gun, Exmoor park
wardens claimed to be seeing not one but two of the black
leopardlike creatures. Was there now a family of beasts to
contend with?

This information caused no surprise to some witnesses, for
over the years a number had reported seeing more than one
big cat. Mr Kingsley-Newman, a South Devon farmer who
had constantly complained of losing stock to a large black cat
on his land, saw one evening when turning into his driveway
not one but two panther-size black cats in the headlights of
his car. One of the animals was calmly drinking from his
cattle trough. It was the last straw for Kingsley-Newman. No
one had believed him when he said he was seeing one cat, and
now he was faced with two! He jumped out of his car and
raced indoors for his gun, determined to shoot the cats and
provide the proof at last of his sightings. When he returned,
only one of the cats remained in sight. He fired, peppering the
wall behind the cat – and presumably the beast itself – with
pellets. The animal retreated at speed round the back of the
farm building, with Kingsley-Newman in hot pursuit. He
cornered the cat in the enclosed space of a partially constructed tractor shed. Then he realised his stupidity. As he
swung his torch beam across he saw the beast crouched on a
beam of the incomplete roof, ready to spring down on him.
Luckily for Mr Kingsley-Newman, the cat had no wish to
prolong the meeting and it leapt over a wall and disappeared
into the darkness.

Witnesses had also reported seeing the Tedburn St Mary
cat with a cub trailing behind it.

In January 1988 the mystery beasts decided against being
so camera shy. The staff working at an electricity sub-station

at Wimple on the outskirts of Exeter and local residents had reported seeing creatures like black panthers the size of Alsatian dogs wandering about the perimeter of the station. Proof of the sightings came when the security cameras around the station picked up one of the pantherlike cats and beamed it back to the control room for the assembled staff to view.

Few beast hunters, however, were offered the comfort of viewing the mystery cats by high-tech. Most were faced with long treks across the freezing wet moorlands, often knee-deep in mud, in an attempt to gain the first clear photographs of the beast. Although summer weather conditions provided less discomfort for searchers, the increased growth of the moorland vegetation made the task more difficult in the warm dry months. A great deal of the moor is covered in bracken, providing perfect cover for a large animal to move about unseen. Even deer and grazing ponies could disappear among the waving fronds. How easy, then, for a sleek feline to make a sinewy passage through the wiry stalks below a broad green canopy, unnoticed by even the most dedicated beast hunter. But in winter the moors are bare, only the dense conifer plantations providing cover for the larger animals. In such bleak conditions the chances of seeing the beast moving about the landscape are greatly increased, even if the comfort of the hunters is correspondingly decreased.

For at least one hunter, the discomfort became positively dangerous. Farmer Peter Baily of Tiverton, in Devon, decided to take matters into his own hands when confronted with a visit from a predator that scaled a six-foot fence before smashing its way into his poultry pen and ripping apart his prize geese. As there had been sightings of a black pantherlike animal in the area, he presumed he had received a visit from the beast and was determined to trap it. He designed and constructed a steel cage with the dimensions of a coffin, and that is what it nearly became – his own.

He had sited the trap in a remote area of the moor. In early February 1991 he was setting a dead pheasant as bait when he accidently sprang the trap with himself inside. For two days he huddled there, freezing in the bitter winter weather, eating the raw bait to survive. He said, afterwards, 'I was terrified and yelled out, but nobody heard me. I had a thick coat on, otherwise I would have frozen to death.'

Peter Bailey's ordeal luckily ended when a passing shepherd found him and released him, but an episode that became a huge joke could so easily have ended in tragedy.

The Exmoor beast had almost claimed its first human victim.

7

Missing Without Trace

If the beast of Exmoor was large, feline and black, it could be a
melanistic jaguar or a leopard, both of which prey on primates
and therefore might consider man to be a legitimate part of their
diet. Why had no one been attacked if there was even one such
beast roaming at will across the British moorlands?

Colin Bath was in charge of mammals at Paignton Zoo
when I was researching *Cat Country* and I talked to him
about the possibility of there being a large black feral cat in
the Tedburn area. In his view it was highly unlikely that
either leopards or jaguars were loose in the British countryside because, if they were, they would have attacked humans.

'A puma, yes,' he said, 'that could live and breed quite
easily and harmlessly in the countryside without drawing
attention to itself. Feeding on rabbits and deer, it would not
be a danger to anyone. A leopard or a jaguar wandering loose
– that is a very different situation. I would quite happily go
into a wood where there was a whole family of pumas living
wild, but you wouldn't get me going within a mile of
anywhere suspected of harbouring either of the others. If
there is a big black feral cat in the Devonshire countryside, it

would have to be either a jaguar or a leopard, more likely a leopard, and it would pose a serious threat to anyone it encountered.'

Both these cats can certainly be mankillers in their own habitat. If one of either species had been hunting for any period in the Devonshire countryside, then someone, somewhere, would have been attacked and either badly mauled or killed. Yet, so far, it hasn't happened, despite the sightings of panther-size cats stretching back for many years.

Or has it?

There is one unsolved mystery involving a missing person in the West Country that could possibly have been the result of an attack by a killer cat. The evidence is purely circumstantial, but the facts fit a sudden and swift attack by a large predator capable of killing and carrying off prey the size of a full grown ewe.

On a pleasant summer's day – Saturday, 19th August 1978 – thirteen-year-old Genette Tate set off to do her evening paper-round in the quiet little South Devon village of Aylesbeare. By 3 p.m. she was riding her bicycle home along Within Lane, a typical hedged and banked winding Devon lane so dreaded by touring motorists and loved by photographers. At a small bridge crossing a narrow stream, Genette met two of her school friends, Tracey Pratt and Margaret Heavey, and she dismounted to walk with them up the small hill, pushing her bike. When the ground levelled out, she remounted, said goodbye to her friends and pedalled round a bend out of sight.

She was never seen again, and her fate has never been discovered. Young Genette Tate had ridden away from her friends and apparently out of this world.

Margaret and Tracey followed Genette around the bend and five minutes later, just three hundred yards from where they had last seen her, they found Genette's bicycle lying on its side in the lane, the back wheel still spinning. A few undelivered newspapers lay scattered around the road where they had fallen from the saddle-bag. It was as if Genette had been snatched from her saddle as she was cycling along. There was no sign of any struggle, no evidence of violence. She had simply vanished without trace.

Where the cycle was discovered the lane opened out into a small lay-by where there were facing farm gates. A short distance away, overlooking the lane, was a row of houses at the edge of a village estate. Anyone, in any of the houses, glancing from an upstairs window, would have had a clear view of the exact spot where Genette disappeared. Unhappily no one did happen to look out at that moment and so no one was able to report on the events of those missing five minutes between the three friends walking together and the two girls finding the abandoned bicycle.

At first the girls thought that Genette was playing a joke on them and hiding behind the hedge. They called to her and searched, quickly tiring of the game. When Genette didn't appear they began to get worried. Finally they decided to wheel the bike back to Genette's house in the hope of finding her there.

Genette's father, John Tate, and her stepmother had gone to Exeter, and when they returned home they found Tracey waiting for them with the bicycle. There was still no sign of Genette and the alarm was raised.

The news spread quickly through the small village and neighbours gathered to help in the search, beginning in the area around Within Lane, hunting through the hedgerows and quartering the surrounding fields where the girl had last been seen. There was always the fear that she had simply fallen off her bike and would be wandering stunned or injured somewhere in the local countryside. The local policeman, Constable Geoffrey Laws, contacted headquarters in Exeter and an official search was started. By the time the police arrived, neighbours of the Tates had already contacted friends and checked out areas around the village where the girl might have gone.

The first line of enquiry was the possibility that the girl had
had an accident on the road, possibly sustaining a head injury
and was now wandering around suffering from concussion or
loss of memory. A more sinister thought was that she had
wandered off confused, that she had sunk into a coma
somewhere and now lay dying or dead. Another suspicion
was that the girl had simply run away from home, maybe as a
joke, perhaps as the result of family friction or home worries.
Most disappearances of children from their homes are the
result of family or school pressure, perhaps an argument at
home, worry about exams or school work, or even violence
in the home or bullying at school.

Most, but not all.

As the police continued their inquiries they became
increasingly concerned. If Genette had run away, it appeared to
have been a decision made on the spur of the moment. She had
taken no extra clothing with her and neither her savings nor the
takings from her newspaper-round had been touched. If she
had chosen to go, she had taken nothing with her but the light
summer clothes she wore, not even a personal memento or a
favourite possession such as a toy or photograph.

The two girls who found the bike had unwittingly
interfered with the evidence by removing it and taking it back
to the village. A careful examination of the site produced no
sign of a struggle and there were no skid marks on the road to
suggest that a car had been involved in Genette's disappearance. The girls said the bike was lying on its side as if
suddenly laid down, but not thrown to the side of the lane.
Forensic experts who examined the machine found no recent
scratches or scrapes to the paintwork and no damage to the
frame, so supporting the story the two girls had told. Yet the
bike, a Christmas present, was known to have been Genette's
pride and joy. Her friends could not imagine her throwing it
down, if she had dismounted for any reason, and not standing
it carefully by the roadside. If she had been the victim of a
hit-and-run driver, how could the bike remain unmarked?

By the end of the first day, although it was early for a full-scale 'missing persons' inquiry to be set up, the police were convinced that something unusual had occurred and they were concerned for the child's safety. An incident centre had been set up in the village hall and police officers and villagers combed the fields and lanes by torchlight until finally the darkness and the weather defeated them.

Over the following days and weeks a police helicopter, mounted police officers, Royal Marines from nearby Lympstone, police tracker dogs and body dogs, together with hundreds of local people, searched the area around Aylesbeare without any result. No clue was discovered to indicate what had occurred in the five minutes before Genette's disappearance.

As one police officer commented, 'It was as if she was suddenly snatched off the face of the earth!'

Who had taken her, where, and why?

As the weeks became months, the summer vegetation died down and searchers, now fearing the worst, expected the shrivelling bracken and falling leaves would reveal Genette's resting place, either the spot to which she had wandered injured to die like a wild animal alone, or else the place to which she had been taken by her abductor and left.

But the denuded winter landscape provided no more clues to the child's whereabouts. The police were baffled.

A child being abducted and murdered is unfortunately not a rare incident in modern times, but it is rare for the body not to be found. When a body is discovered, forensic evidence is discovered with it – clues to where the crime was committed and to the person responsible for it, often just fibres of cloth, hairs, stains for genetic matching – small fragments that put together a picture of the last hours or minutes of the victim's life, and sometimes an identity to the killer. Without a body, the detective's work is much more difficult, although the place where the victim was last seen can provide vital information such as tyre tracks, footprints, eye-witness descriptions that can help to pinpoint the killer. In the case of little Genette Tate, the police had nothing.

Holidaymakers who had spoken to Margaret and Tracey moments before the missing girl joined them were traced and interviewed. The two girls had been only three hundred yards from the abandoned bike, just minutes away from Genette when whatever happened to her took place. Yet no one had seen anything unusual. Nor on a quiet, warm summer's day, when sound should carry, had anything been heard – no car revving up, no screech of brakes, no raised voices, no scream nor shout for help.

A car that was never traced had passed the witnesses in the lane travelling in the direction in which Genette had gone. Was it possible for a stranger to stop a car alongside Genette, open a door, grab her off her bicycle, throw her forcibly into the vehicle and speed off within three hundred yards of witnesses with no one hearing so much as a car door slam or a muffled cry.

Certainly children have been snatched in this way but usually the driver slows down, stops, strikes up a conversation, perhaps asking for directions, then attempts to entice the potential victim into the car and, having succeeded, slams the door and drives off at speed. Certainly the whole episode could have taken place within the time limit but it was hard to believe that the two holidaymakers or Genette's two friends would have heard no sound of any kind, even if they did not associate it with the events at the time but only in retrospect.

To reinforce the evidence that there had been no unusual noises in the lane that August afternoon, all four witnesses were subjected to examination while under hypnosis. Margaret and Tracey retraced their steps on that fateful day, reliving their last conversation with Genette, and the few minutes between their friend cycling away ahead of them and their finding the bike lying in the road. Even under hypnosis neither girl recalled any sound that would suggest a struggle or a car involved in an incident occurring just a few yards ahead of them.

Silently and swiftly, a young girl had vanished without trace. As her father, John Tate, later wrote in his book *Genette, Where Is She Now?*, 'If Genette had run away, we couldn't help remembering that at the beginning of her paper-round Genette crossed a main bus route. If she had decided to run off, wasn't that the logical point for her to make good her escape, and not halfway down a quiet country lane?'

It was also difficult to explain why, when her family was away for the day, the girl would do her paper-round before running off in such a dramatic manner. After all, with her family out of the way, she could have prepared for her journey in comfort, packing whatever she needed before she left.

So far, fifteen years after the event, the mystery of Genette's disappearance remains unsolved, despite the police continuing to make periodic inquiries, the involvement of numerous clairvoyants (including the respected Dutch medium, Croiset) and the girl's family persisting with their own almost obsessive search for clues.

While I was researching my book *Cat Country*, two years after Genette had vanished, I decided to follow up the possibility that some of the mysterious big black cats seen could have been feral leopards. As experts constantly assured me that feral leopards were very dangerous and would attack humans, I began to look into cases of missing persons or mysterious deaths to see if any could have been the result of a big cat attack. Of all the cases I examined, that of young Genette Tate proved to be the most likely. Over the years there had been reports of big cats seen in the area of Woodbury Common and the place was within easy reach of both Exmoor and Dartmoor. A big cat might well have a hunting range of a hundred miles. My only sources, however, were press reports, and often the police withold the identity of a suspect when there is a lack of clear evidence. Although the police had stated they were baffled by the girl's disappearance, it was possible that they had a very good idea of exactly what had happened to Genette and who had been involved, but they did not have enough evidence to stand up in court. An example of such a situation was a series of killings in London in the 1960s. Nicknamed 'Jack the Stripper' because he preyed on prostitutes and left their bodies stripped of clothing, the killer was never named. Yet in Scotland Yard there is a bulky file naming a prime suspect in the case, who died suddenly in rather strange circumstances that have never themselves been explained and the police immediately closed their file on Jack the Stripper. Officially the killer has never been found. With the suspect's untimely death, the killings ceased, so supporting the police's suspicions as to the identity of the murderer. But because the man could no longer be tried for the crimes and because making their suspicions public knowledge would only harm an innocent, already bereaved and confused family, the police remained silent about the results of their investigations.

It was possible that such a situation existed in the Genette Tate case, that there was a suspect about whom the police had insufficient evidence to act. If there were such a suspect, then I could remove Genette from my very short list of possible cat attacks.

I decided to confront the police and explain my interest. I expected to receive an immediate brush-off which would suggest they were not so baffled as they publicly claimed. As it happened, I was not dismissed and detectives agreed to take me around the area where Genette had disappeared to see if I could come to any conclusions. This alone persuaded me that they did not have a suspect or any idea of what had happened to Genette on that August afternoon.

I had never been to Aylesbeare before and had no clear picture of the type of countryside in which the girl had vanished. I was driven along Within Lane, past the house where Genette had made her last paper delivery. It was summer and the vegetation was high, the trees in full leaf, just as they had been on the day of her disappearance. We reached the point in the lane where Genette had met her friends and then crossed the bridge where she was last seen. A stream ran under the bridge and through a densely wooded gully. The lane was narrow and winding, a typical Devon lane, bordered by a high dense thicket hedge that made visibility impossible from the road to the woods and fields on either side – until we reached the spot where the bicycle had been found lying in the road, its wheel still spinning. There the lane opened out into a crossroads, farm gates leading to rough tracks on either side of the lane giving vision directly across the sloping fields to the hills on one side and to a row of cottages at the edge of the village on the other. It was the first exposed spot along that section of the lane and, being overlooked by houses, seemed the least likely spot for someone to stage an attack on a randomly chosen victim.

The policeman left me there to explore the area. I climbed over the gate on the village side and walked back towards the wooded area that skirted the stream. It was a fairly narrow wood, consisting mainly of virtually impregnable blackthorn thickets that certainly could not have been searched during the hunt for the missing girl. The branches were tangled old wood of many years growth. The police and searchers had been looking at areas where the girl herself could walk or someone could enter, dragging or carrying her, and the wooded area could be eliminated because it was obvious that no one had entered the area for years. I entered it by crawling under the spiny blackthorn branches, wriggling my way through small tunnels made by passing mammals. Once inside it was easier to move around and there was plenty of evidence of fox, badger and roe deer, the trees providing protection, the stream providing drinking-water. It was an ideal spot for a big cat to lie up in if passing through, though not a large enough wood to provide a home territory. I followed the easiest route through the trees, gradually striking out up the slope to reach high ground and the edge of the thicket. Leaving the trees at a natural break giving easy

11 Stripped sheep carcass showing peeled away skin and undamaged ribs typical of a big cat kill.
12 Mystery grey feline photographed by Steve Joyce on Tonmawr hillside.
13 Black catlike animal photographed on the same hillside six months later.
(Photo: Anne Maggs)

14, 15   The cub of the black Tonmawr cat, photographed by Steve Joyce.

16   Taxidermist's preservation of the first Kellas cat specimen.

17, 18   The author's own pair of Kellas cats. The female (*right*) gave birth to three kittens in May 1992.

19   The Dufftown cat (*below right*).

20 The head of the Dufftown cat, an adult male which differs from both the Kellas cat and the domestic cat, with a small brain, a powerful jaw and unusual dentition.

21 The skull of a Kellas cat (right) and the skull of a Dufftown cat showing the smaller cranial capacity.

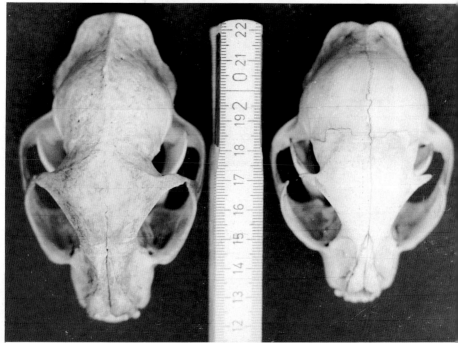

passage, I broke through to the open hillside and looked down. My line of vision went precisely down to the two gates at the point in the lane where Genette's bicycle was found. Had I been a hunting big cat, I would almost certainly have left the wood at about that point and I would have looked directly across the open hillside to the field on the other side of the lane where sheep were grazing. If I was viewing the sheep as potential prey, then I would have run in a straight line down the slope, leapt over the gate at that exact point, crossed the lane in a single bound, sprung over the opposite gate and been in the field of sheep in seconds, once again hidden from the road.

I sat down on the grass and tried to visualise the scene two years previously. What if a hunting cat had been passing through and had stood on the hillside that afternoon, eyeing the sheep hungrily? What if it had decided to make an attack, had bounded down the hill towards the obvious crossing point, when suddenly an animal had appeared moving up the lane? Not a walking, upright human of the sort the cat had learnt to avoid, but an animal the size of a deer or a sheep, travelling on all fours, its head bent forward, its sloping back an inviting target? Yet not a sheep or a deer but a young girl, bent forward, riding her bike? A swift leap over the gate, a grab, a second leap over the opposite gate carrying its prey and away? No sound, no voices raised, no car, no body. Just a bicycle lying tumbled in the road, its wheels still spinning, papers scattered for her friends to find.

There is no way in which to prove that such an attack took place. Any physical evidence would have vanished long ago, rotted, removed by scavangers, or blown on the wind. Only the discovery of Genette's whereabouts, or the finding of her killer, could prove that it had not. But the hypothesis made sense of the known facts.

The area was ideal for an attack by a wild animal but it was not a likely spot for a human attacker to choose, especially overlooked by houses. If the attacker had been the man driving the car that passed the two girls and the holiday-makers, he would have known that people were nearby. Would he really be certain that he could succeed in stopping the car, grabbing Genette, preventing her from uttering a scream, getting either her struggling form, or her body into the car and making his getaway within the few minutes he had before the girls he knew were following would arrive at the scene? The risks were surely far too great, and he would have continued his journey until he encountered a more suitable victim. And as John Tate pointed out, surely the bike would have been tossed aside into the hedge, either to avoid obstructing the car or else to hide the evidence of the attack.

Everything fitted the circumstances of an animal attack, but I needed to be certain of two things. Had there been sheep in both fields on the day in question or in only one? If sheep had been in both fields, then it was unlikely that a cat would cross the lane from one to the other to hunt. I checked up with the police officers who had been involved in the search immediately following Genette's disappearance. They remembered quite clearly that cattle had been grazing in the field next to the wood, sheep in the opposite field, just as they were on the day of my visit. Also I asked if the handlers had noticed any unusual reaction by the dogs during the search of the area? The police had been looking for human scent, but had the dogs showed any sign of picking up another, more frightening scent? Dogs normally showed fear on scenting the big cats.

I was amazed to learn that it had been three days before the body dogs had been brought in to search the area. They would have been in plenty of time to discover a body hidden in the undergrowth of course, but the remains of cat prey?

What is known certainly does not rule out a cat attack. Genette was small and light for her age, certainly the size that a cat could carry away with comparative ease, a cat species of the size of a leopard that can carry an antelope up a tree or a sheep deep into forestry. There are records of Africans riding bicycles being attacked by leopards mistaking their crouched shape for a running animal.

If the unfortunate young girl had been the victim of such an attack, it is doubtful she would ever have been aware of what was happening. She would have been bent over her bike, concentrating on the road ahead, perhaps thinking of her sister going on holiday or what she would be having for tea. Normal everyday thoughts, then suddenly nothing! No pain, no fear. The cat would have struck from behind, almost certainly breaking her neck instantly, there would have been no time to cry out, no realisation of what was happening, just an instant and painless death.

For Genette's sake I hope that, if she is dead, she died in such a way. Not a victim of rape, not abducted by a perverted twisted human being who could cause her pain and fear before she died. Simply a victim of mistaken identity and the harsh law of nature.

Her death would not even suggest that the cat had been an intended mankiller. Her white shirt, her size and shape – to the predator she would have appeared to be a sheep. There is no reason to fear that such a sequence of events could ever again be repeated.

It was five years after Genette's disappearance that *Cat Country* was published and the marines from the same barracks as those who had searched Woodbury Common for any sign of the young girl, were hunting through the Devon countryside for sheep-killing leopard-size wild cats. I did not write about my research into the Genette Tate case in 1982 for fear that the thought of her being a victim of a big cat might distress her family. But as the years have passed with no further evidence of Genette's fate being discovered, I hope that the idea of an instant painless death is far less upsetting than murder, and may dispel the nightmares of her suffering before her death, if, indeed, she is dead.

There the speculation has to stop. Only the discovery of

Genette alive and well, or else her grave, can solve the mystery, and either event becomes increasingly unlikely.

When I stood on the hillside on the outskirts of Aylesbeare that summer afternoon, wondering if two years previously a large feline predator had stood at the same spot, few people believed that leopard-size cats could be roaming wild in the British Isles. Years later, as I write this chapter, many people, once sceptics, now believe in the existence of the big cats, even if their origins and species are still shrouded in mystery.

If the cats exist, then one could have prowled around the village of Aylesbeare in August 1978 and Genette could have fallen a victim to its predatory behaviour.

Perhaps discovering the identity of the Exmoor beast will in turn solve another strange mystery of the West Country.

8

A Living Fossil

Despite all the eye-witness accounts, we still do not know to which species the Exmoor beast belongs. It would appear that there are more beasts than one in North Devon and that similar predators hunt across the whole of the British Isles. We have built up a picture of their size, how they live, their territory, their eating habits and even breeding behaviour. There are a few hazy photographs, a couple of recordings of catlike screams, numerous plaster casts of paw prints taken from Cornwall to Caithness, and mountains of dead and eaten sheep.

The most important evidence comes from the many descriptions of the cats by people who have encountered them unexpectedly in lonely rural areas – people from all walks of life, including vets, doctors and police officers. Yet, as Sergeant Goodman of the South Molton police pointed out, witnesses seldom, if ever, identify the species of cat they have seen. They can liken it to a black panther, or a puma perhaps, but never name a precise species.

Why?

Is it because what is seen has no exact comparison among

the few known big cat species in the world today? Those species are quite distinct from each other, so why is it so difficult for witnesses to pick out which cat they have seen? Certainly the leopard, the cheetah and the jaguar are golden-coated spotted cats, but there are distinct differences in size and shape, and so each should be easily distinguishable. Even the similarities between these three do not explain the difficulty, for witnesses of the British big cat never report seeing yellow cats with black spots.

If the sightings are of escapees, why are there no yellow spotted cats among them when that is the most common colour found among the big cats today? In modern times, perhaps, but what of the distant past? Which other species of cats once roamed the British Isles and what happened to them? The truth is we do not actually know how many species of cats once hunted across this island; we know only of those that have left us a fossil record.

The Oligocene period, when cats first appeared, began thirty-six million years ago. A time traveller from now to then would recognise a number of plants and creatures that have been around for the intervening years. When the dinosaurs ruled the earth in the Cretaceous period, 140 million years ago, the great reptiles also shared the vast humid swamps and forests with the frogs, salamanders, snakes, lizards, turtles and crocodiles that we see today. These survivors are what we call living fossils, creatures recognisable today that can also be found in fossil form millions of years old. There are also survivors among the flora of this planet. A walk in the forests of the Tertiary period, some sixty-five million years ago, would have found many trees that can still be seen today, such as banana, palm, fig, redwoods, oak, sycamore and ginkgo, to name but a few. Some fifty-five million years ago, at the beginning of the Eocene, there were breadfruit, willow, walnut, birch, alder, hickory, maple and ash trees. Lemurs clung to the branches and woodpeckers, owls, vultures, herons and cranes took to the air, while ducks, gulls, petrels, cormorants and divers bobbed about the seas and lakes. And within the waters fish such as sturgeon were joined by terrapins, and on land iguanas, monitors and slow-worms slithered or darted after crickets, grasshoppers, termites, cockroaches, beetles, dragonflies, glow-worms and bluebottles.

By the Oligocene period and the arrival of the cats, we already had many living fossils. Hedgehogs, moles, shrews and the ancestor of the Sumatra rhino can be added to the list. Many of the early cats were strange-looking beasts to our modern eyes. Nature was experimenting to evolve the most successful of all hunters. Some were heavy and clumsy animals, relying on weight and power to catch their prey; others, such as the early sabre-tooths, developing strange weapons. A few, however, were like our modern cats, leopard-size and with teeth like those seen in big cats today.

By twenty-five million years ago, the cats had become the most successful of predators, and then the first apes appeared, together with a small cat the size of the modern European wildcat – tiny when compared with the lion-size sabre-tooth Machaerodus, this cat genus Felis was to be the most successful of all the felines, and is the ancestor of all our modern cats.

As the cats evolved, so the hominid Ramapithecus spread from the African continent, cats and man developing side by side as the Pleistocene or the Ice Age brought a series of devastating winters and summers lasting three million years. With the rise of man went the destruction of many of the cat species. There were five long winters, each lasting thousands of years, the changing climate destroying many species. The newly emerging man and the cats, however, adapted and survived.

Just eleven thousand years ago the huge and grotesque sabre-tooth Smilodon still hunted across the American Continent, evidence of his numbers suggested by the two and a half thousand fossils unearthed around the famous La Brea tar pits in Los Angeles. Obviously attracted by the struggles of trapped animals, the hunters themselves fell prey to the grip of the tar beds.

Smilodon was not the largest cat to hunt the new continent however. *Panthera atrox*, the American Lion, was a quarter again as large as the biggest tiger today, a huge predator built for speed as well as power, with a formidable bite but without the exaggerated dentition of the sabre-tooths. A close relative to this cat was the cave-lion, the first of the early cats which we can reconstruct to include colour and fur, for early man has left us beautifully painted pictures of the creature they feared and hunted on the cave walls of the disputed territory. The cave-lion is shown as maneless and sometimes striped.

Other cats were recorded that are still with us today – the lynx, the leopard and the cheetah hunted alongside early man two million years ago, although their range is greatly reduced in modern times – but were there species of which we have no record that hunted the grasslands and forests?

The process of extinction during this period lasted between one and twenty thousand years, depending on the area, during which an average of fifty per cent of known species were destroyed. This is a very short time span, considering that they had survived millions of years of climatic change and geological upheaval, it took a comparatively short time for them to disappear.

The cause of their destruction is thought to be linked to the evolution of the ape-like creature, man. Even *Smilodon* and the American Lion had no chance against the weak and puny animal with the greater brain. The destruction took on two basic forms: direct, through rivalry, and indirect, through interference with the food chain.

The direct method involved hunting and killing the beasts that posed a threat to a man as a species, by including man as part of the food chain and also as a rival for the same prey animals and the same sheltering caves.

Man did not have the impressive teeth of *Smilodon*, nor the speed and power of the American Lion, but he had the ability to plan and to scheme, hunting in a pack, using guile and cunning rather than brute force. If nature had not provided him with formidable natural weapons, it had given him the means to manufacture artificial substitutes. Thousands of years ago, the world saw the beginning of the mass destruction of numerous species, including the mammoth, woolly rhino, giant deer, cave-lion, cave-panther, cave-bear, cave-hyaena and scimitar cat, to name just a few in a list that sadly continues to grow until the present day.

And these are the known species. How many more were destroyed leaving no visible evidence of ever having existed? Without the survival of fossil remains or cave paintings, we have no way of knowing just how many strange and magnificent creatures roamed the earth at the same time as our early ancestors.

The life-style of some creatures ensured a record of their existence, the environment of swamp and cave-dwellers providing the possibility of fossilisation as their remains were covered in silt, mud or soil. The remains of forest and savanna-dwellers would have been swiftly dismembered and eaten by scavengers, leaving behind no record. It is no coincidence that we have a number of fossils of the cave-lion but few of the forest and grassland cats. The huge number of specimens of *Smilodon* found can be explained by the unusual ground conditions of the tar pits.

When did most of the big cats of the British Isles become extinct? Certainly more than ten thousand years ago. But if we have no knowledge of all the species that once hunted across these islands, can we be sure they are all extinct?

The idea of an unknown species of big cat lurking in the forests and woodlands of Britain may seem impossible, but is it? Could an animal keep itself hidden from its natural enemy – man – for thousands of years, preying on deer and grazing sheep, hunting in the wild lonely places at night, avoiding its only predator, *Home sapiens*?

The scientists might shake their heads, but all the evidence would suggest that it is indeed possible.

From Cornwall to Caithness people are reporting sightings of large mystery cats. Farmers across the land are complaining of losing stock to powerful unidentified predators, predators that can kill a heavy ewe so swiftly that the attacked animal will die with unchewed grass still in its mouth. It is no small predator that can devour enormous quantities of meat from a carcase overnight, leaving a tidy stripped skeleton with very little damage to the bones. It is a strong predator that can carry, not drag, a full-grown ewe a distance of miles, crossing hedges, streams, and fences without effort.

Everything points to a powerful catlike predator that hunts mainly at night, a predator that is frequently seen but never clearly identified by witnesses – a big cat, but of many colours; black, like a black panther; brown, like a puma; but also mottled, grey, dark brown, tabby and russet red. And if this diversity of coloration is not confusing enough, there are even variations on these colours – black with light-colour chests or feet; cream, fawn or gold with brown patches or bands; light grey or fawn with distinct spots and stripes – colours that are not found on any of the known species of modern big cats.

Certainly there could be escaped pumas or black leopards living feral in the British Isles, although not as many as the sightings would suggest. There could be the odd hybrid surviving in the countryside. We know that big cats will mate between species, but these hybrids are normally sterile.

The mystery cats might not be recognisable when compared to known species, but witnesses appear to be describing similar beasts across the whole country.

When describing the Exmoor beast Andy Wilkins had said, 'The animal was big, Great Dane size, standing a couple of inches above the knee. It was long bodied with thick-set powerful shoulders, almost no neck and a squat, ugly, quite small round head with pricked ears.'

Colonel WAC Haines of Brushford described a big catlike animal near Witheridge, Devon, in 1969. He said it was the size of a calf, with a brown head, large black prominent eyes and a nose 'extraordinarily like a pug. Its left ear was pricked but the other hung down as if torn. Its ribs were a bright pale chestnut turning to a sort of dirty gingery-brown and its hindquarters were darker still. On its hindquarters were three black spots about the size of a penny and along its spine was a ridge of hair about two inches in length which waved in the breeze. Its body was smooth-haired and thin. Its tail long and thin, looked like a piece of dirty rope. Its legs were very long for its body and pale fawn in colour.'

He had been driving along the road in brilliant sunshine when he spotted the animal on the roadside. He watched it from a distance of about fifteen feet for about three minutes. Certainly the animal he described is not to be found in the natural history books, but could he have been mistaken?

Perhaps. Yet in 1983 police officers in Stokenchurch, in Buckinghamshire, were hunting a slender feline the size of an Alsatian, deep fawn in colour with merging black spots on its back.

In North-east Scotland in 1988 Mrs Linda Brody was driving along a road when she encountered a huge black cat on the roadside. She described it as the size of a Great Dane, but much heavier. She stopped alongside the seated cat and studied it from the safety of her car for a few minutes before the animal bounded off. She said it was a terrifying beast with large prominent eyes but a fairly small head in contrast to its broad body. It seemed to have no neck, the muscle on the back of its neck merging into the shoulders, almost like a hump. It had heavy jowls and a large broad, almost puglike nose.

It is not difficult to find similarities between the animal sighted in Scotland and the animal seen on Exmoor by the Royal Marine Commandos. The colour is different but there are facial similarities between the pug-faced black animal and the creature seen earlier by Colonel Haines in Devon. There are also colour similarities between Colonel Haines's animal and the brown creature with merging spots seen at Stokenchurch. Certainly Colonel Haines saw a very thin long-legged animal, but it also appears to have been rather tatty. Could it have been thinner than the other animals sighted simply because it was either ill or very old?

None of these animals exactly matches any known species of big cat, yet all the witnesses are certain the animals were feline rather than canine.

Of course some sightings are confused because they take place in poor light, or at night, in car headlights or by torch beam. But some animals are seen in daylight and are studied for up to twenty minutes by multiple witnesses, and some of the witnesses have been rangers, farmers, gamekeepers, all experienced in the study of wildlife. Others have been trained observers, such as policemen and armed services personnel. If only a small percentage of the sightings are correct, then a number of large catlike animals are roaming the British Isles, and if just some of the descriptions are accurate, then the animals appear to belong to no known species.

The few photographs taken of the mystery animals would suggest that the witnesses are not mistaken in their confusion. The leopard-size black cat that I photographed in Wales (opposite page 55) is unfortunately too distant to show many features. Even its size cannot easily be determined, but no one has actually attempted to gauge it. An arched branch of gorse in the picture provides a very good size comparison, but the authorities and scientists who claimed the cat could have been a domestic cat made no attempt to go to the Welsh hillside and examine the vegetation that can be seen in the photograph. Seven years later I went back to Wales and photographed the branch that was still there, after which I removed it from the site before it rotted away.

The only close-up photograph of a mystery cat to exist at the time of writing is that of the cub of the black animal taken by Steve Joyce in his garden at the foot of the hill. (See pages 86–7.) Again the authorities dismissed the photograph as that of a domestic cat or a wildcat.

Closer examination of the profile of the cub taking bait is extremely revealing. Although taken at night with a low-powered flashlight, the photograph still shows some very interesting features when compared to a domestic cat photographed in a similar situation. The cub is obviously much larger and longer in the body than the domestic cat. The shoulders are very muscular, the back of the neck showing a pronounced hump. The ears are large and set back on the comparatively small head. The top of the skull is elongated and broad, the nose appearing almost snub. The lower jaw is quite heavy and the canine teeth pronounced.

It is easy to understand how a larger adult version of the same shape would appear so bulky around the shoulders that it could be described as having no neck – a description frequently given to the mystery cats, including the beast of Exmoor. The most interesting feature of the cublike animal, however, is the extended front paw grabbing the bait.

A number of prints found at the scene of big cat sightings or sheep kills have shown a distinctive feature. The front paws appear to have graded pads, rather like a hand with different size fingers. (See pages 86–7.) There is a large pad rather like a thumb, the heel pad showing a lop-sided shape to accommodate this big toe, and while the centre two toes are fairly evenly matched, the fourth toe is very small, almost resembling a little finger on a hand.

Modern cats, including the domestic moggie, and such big cats as the lion and the tiger, have the same basic foot pattern. The halfmoon heel pad has the four toes of even size arranged around it. Although a cat can grasp with a hand-like movement, the toes are all the same length, appearing to be different due to the way in which they are set round the half-circle of the heel pad.

In the Steve Joyce photograph the mystery cub would

appear to have a very different foot structure. The toes seem to be set across the paw like the fingers on a human hand, the centre toes long, the toe nearer the camera much shorter and smaller than the other two. The far toe is obscured from view but it also appears shorter than the centre two toes. Although the foot appears to be most unusual, it would certainly make sense of the graded pad footprints found at the scene of big cat sightings or sheep kills.

The head and general appearance of the cub certainly resembles a puma, but the coloration cannot be found on any modern big cat. If the photograph is genuine, then it would appear to show an unknown species of feline. As I saw the cub myself on the hillside, running with the black pantherlike cat that I took to be its mother, I know that Steve Joyce's photograph is genuine, but only a careful study of the picture can decide other people.

Another photograph taken by Steve Joyce shows a strange grey cat with a white or light chest. (See pages 86–7.) The animal has very powerful hind quarters and a muscular neck and shoulders. The head is small and the face flat. The animal is seated above a stump that measured two feet high, giving a rough scale for size.

The cat was photographed a short distance from the garden to which the cublike animal was attracted by bait and on the same hillside where I had photographed the black pantherlike cat. It is possible that the grey animal is the father of the cub. Six months earlier Mr and Mrs Dil Maggs reported seeing a huge and very ugly grey striped cat the size of a lion crossing the road in front of their Range Rover.

That three large cats of different colours and sizes could be reported and photographed on the same hillside within a period of six months suggests that other witnesses claiming the same variety of sightings in other areas are in fact telling the truth. Yet there are no known species of large grey cats with white or light fronts, with or without stripes.

The black cat I photographed certainly could be a black

leopard, but its graded footprint is unlike that of any known big cat. And although I cannot prove it, I saw it running with the cublike animal to be seen in Steve Joyce's photograph. As the sites can be identified, however, it can be proved that the three mystery cats were photographed on the same hillside. Six months later Anne Maggs spotted the big black cat again, photographing it as it moved into the rushes below the gorse bushes where I had seen and photographed it the previous spring.

The mystery that surrounds the Exmoor beast is obviously not unique. Similar sightings and the same confusion can be discovered across the whole of the British Isles. But if an unknown big cat species is living wild in Britain, where has it come from?

9

The Cat of the Baskervilles

The most persistent stumbling block in the scientific mind when considering the hypothesis that the mystery cats could be an unknown species, a living and unrecorded fossil, is the argument that if the creatures have existed for thousands of years why have they not been reported before this century?

It is a valid question. However secretive and shy a wild animal may be, it cannot remain completely hidden from the inhabitants that share its territory. If the mystery cats are a species that have existed for thousands of years in an island environment, surely they would have been seen occasionally as their territory became more densely populated by man.

With the aid of electricity, powerful torches, and, most important of all, car headlights, it is not difficult to understand the sudden surge of sightings in the twentieth century, yet it is hard to accept that no farmer or gamekeeper in the few hundred years before 1900 noticed leopard-size cats roaming around the countryside. Or, at least, no such sighting was recorded. But if big cats have escaped notice, historians have been intrigued by the folklore of Black Dog legends to be found across the British Isles.

Black Dogs were believed to be supernatural creatures, monstrous black hounds that haunted the wild and lonely places, terrifying the unfortunate travellers who encountered the ghostly apparitions along the roadside. Clergymen believed them to be companions of the Devil, hell-hounds roaming the earth in search of souls for their master.

I have always been curious to know why the hell-hounds were so frightening to the terrified witnesses. After all, even today, black domestic dogs can frequently be found taking an unaccompanied evening walk along the country lanes. In centuries past many dogs must have been living feral and, before rabies was eliminated from this country, an encounter with a wild dog could have been very dangerous, resulting in a very painful death. Yet it was not a physical but a supernatural fear that sent witnesses hot-foot to the nearest church for protection and help.

I wrote of my research into Black Dog legends in *Cat Country* in 1982, concluding that the evidence suggested the *Hound of the Baskervilles* should be in fact the Cat of the Baskervilles. Then, in September 1989, Brian Duffy wrote an article for the *Daily Express* which was headlined: 'Howling Beast is back in village of the Baskervilles'.

Hill farmers in the Black Mountains of Wales were patrolling their flocks at night in an attempt to protect them from a mysterious predator. Farmer Geoffrey Phillips said, 'The destroyed sheep have cost me many hundreds of pounds. Their throats were torn and their insides ripped out. It was appalling. We have no idea what kind of beast it is. All we know is that the animal is ferocious and we will keep up our guard.'

A local vet commented, 'The wounds inflicted on the sheep were not those that any dog – no matter how big – would inflict. No dog would go on to cause the other internal injuries after first attacking the sheep by the throat.'

It was a puzzle that a number of other veterinary surgeons

had encountered in other parts of the country. But, if not a dog, what kind of creature was it?

The only clues to the identity of the mystery predator were reports of frightening howling carried on the wind down to the tiny hamlet of Clyro, in Powys.

Clyro had once been visited by Sir Arthur Conan Doyle, author of the famous Sherlock Holmes detective stories. The writer had been fascinated by the legend of the Black Hound of Hardwidge, a massive hell-hound that prowled the local hills, killing livestock and terrifying the local inhabitants. He adapted the folktale, changing the location to Dartmoor in Devon, but keeping the local Clyro name of the local Baskerville Hall for his most famous Holmes tale, *The Hound of the Baskervilles*.

In 1989 the local inhabitants were discussing whether the black beast of Hardwidge had returned to hunt the surrounding hills. The modern world had not diluted the superstitious fears of past centuries.

When I suggested in 1982 that the Conan Doyle story should have been called the Cat rather than the Hound of the Baskervilles, I was referring to the hundreds of stories across the country of legendary black dogs and devil hounds whose description frequently suggested feline rather than canine origins. The recent events in the tiny Welsh village have done nothing to suggest otherwise.

Fortunately we have a number of eye-witness accounts from the past, recorded by clergymen of the time, taken directly from the terrified witnesses who had rushed to the church for salvation after encountering the ferocious black beasts across the fields and woods of Britain. We have the Reverend Edmund Jones of Tranch Newport to thank for some of the best documented sightings in his collection of stories entitled, *A Relation of Apparitions of Spirits in the County of Monmouth and the Principality of Wales*, published in 1813.

One story was related to him by 'R.A., a true living experimental Christian'. The Reverend recorded:

As she was going to Laugharn Town, Carmarthenshire, one evening on some business, it being late, her mother dissuaded her from going, telling her it was late and that she would be benighted; likely she might be terrified by an apparition which was both heard and seen by many and by her father amongst others, at a place called Pant y Madog, which was a pit by the side of the lane leading to Laugharn, filled with water and not quite dry in the summer.

However she seemed not to be afraid, therefore went to Laugharn. On coming back before night, though it was rather dark, she passed by the place; but not without thinking of the apparition: but being a little beyond this pit, in a field where there was a little rill of water and just going to pass it, having one foot stretched over it and looking before her, she saw something like a great Dog, one of the Dogs of Hell, coming towards her; being within four or five yards of her it stopped, sat down and set up a scream so horrible, so loud and so strong, that she thought the earth moved under her; with which she fainted.

Obviously the witness was already programmed with the suggestion that she would be most likely to encounter a hell-hound if she followed that route, but it is interesting to note that 'she saw something like a great dog'. This suggests that the animal was different from a normal canine breed. Or perhaps it was not a dog at all. Even the marines on Exmoor, with their sophisticated night sights, were at first unclear if the animal they had seen was dog or cat. How much more difficult it would be for a girl already filled with superstitious dread, using only the flickering light of a candle lantern, or even the natural moonlight, to identify the creature she was seeing.

The site is of interest. 'In a field where there was a little rill of water.' This suggests that she encountered a flesh and blood animal about to take a drink rather than a ghostly apparition floating around the ether. A number of these sightings were recorded in the vicinity of water. Folklore researchers, noting this, came to various conclusions, including that electrical impulses from running water produced the phenomenon or that the water courses were linked with ley lines. No one ever seemed to have suspected that the sightings, or at least some of them, were simply the result of carnal animals taking a nightly drink at the nearest watering-place.

The behaviour of the creature that so terrified the God-fearing girl is also very catlike: 'It stopped, sat down and set up such a scream, so horrible, so loud and so strong.' A dog would be more likely to remain standing if unsettled or annoyed. A cat will set its hindquarters down in a sitting position when contemplating whether to crouch ready for pouncing on a victim or else to retreat, only the lashing tail indicative of its uncertainty of mood. A dog in a similar situation will stand firmly, its head lowered, its lip curled to show its teeth, but with its mouth closed. A cat will frequently sit up and pull backwards, emitting a loud scream of annoyance, or spitting. While a dog will lower its head, lift its hunched shoulder and growl or bark, it will not scream.

Another Black Dog story from Wales was related by Ethel Rudkin who collected folklore stories. Again this was sited by water. It originated from the 1830s and was told by the witness's grandson in 1936.

At Redhill, four miles from Haverfordwest, at a point where a small brook, the Keystone, crosses the Mathry Road to join the Western Cleddau. On the northern side of the little bridge over the brook towards a rather dense growth of trees crowning a miniature cliff. Some three miles further north is the little village of Camrose. At the time of the described incident, my grandfather was the acting steward of the considerable estate of Cambrose and his journeys to the neighbouring town of Haverfordwest were fairly frequent and always on foot. So far as I recollect the story, it was on his way home from Haverfordwest in the darkening evening that he became somewhat alarmed by a considerable commotion in the wood. In his pastoral mind, this could only be caused by a battle royal between some domestic animals and he wondered whose bull had invaded the territory of his neighbour and what dogs were joining in the mêlée. However, he was secure enough in the protection of the hedges and it seemed unlikely that the strife would culminate in the vanquished being forced through the thick trees to a drop over the crest of the little cliff into the brook beneath. A few yards walking brought him to the bridge and here he was terrified to see a huge black dog rise over the trees with a frightful roar and swoop downwards within a few feet of him, to the stream beyond the bridge.

It is difficult to believe that a dog could perform such a feat of elevation, but a feline can clear ten to eleven feet from a ground position with comparative ease. To spring down from a tree would present no problems to a cat. The battle described could have been a territorial dispute, or it could have been simply mating behaviour, which most cats perform with an over abundance of raucous noise.

Other parts of the British Isles have different names for their dogs, usually attempting to describe the sounds made by the various creatures. Lancashire has two names for its demon hounds, Shrieker or Trash – Shrieker because of the terrible screams the creature makes, and Trash because its footsteps are believed to sound like heavy shoes splashing along a muddy road. Both descriptions seem to be more in keeping with feline behaviour than canine, even the sounds of Trash is suggestive of a big cat panting as it prowls. The noise leopards make is sometimes described as sawing wood.

The black dogs also have a fairly close territory, usually woodland. Early in this century a youth who cycled regularly from Leverton to Wrangle reported he 'often saw the Black Dog rush out of a drove-end behind him and lope along to another lane which it turned down.'

It is difficult to understand why the witness did not simply presume it to be a pet or a farm dog out for its normal morning walk. Perhaps the lope gives us a clue. The word would describe the movement of a cat rather than a dog.

Other Black Dogs of regular habits number among them one seen at Bourne Wood that always disappeared 'at a certain handgate at a corner of the wood', and the Dog of Moortown Hall near South Valley that 'always appeared in the hedge at the same place'. The Black Dog of South Kelsey was always sighted walking along a road adjacent to a small plantation and one at Algarkirk was invariably seen near a particular clump of trees. The Dog of Willoughton was usually spotted along a stretch of road beside a fishpond and always disappeared by a particular ash-tree, one witness swearing the animal actually vanished 'up the tree or into the tree'.

As the average lifespan for a domestic dog is fifteen years, less for the larger breeds, and the sightings spanned many years, it is impossible to suppose that reports were of the same single animal living in that area and taking its normal territorial morning walks. The reason why male dogs cock their legs so frequently is to scent-mark their territory, though they do range beyond their boundaries, and the marking is intended to indicate their passage rather than deter other dogs from following. This is typical pack behaviour. Wild cats, however, are solitary hunters, and not only live on average many years longer than dogs, but mark the boundaries of their territory for the specific purpose of warning other felines not to trespass on their areas. When an old cat dies or is evicted from its territory by a younger feline, then it is possible that the newcomer takes over the territory as a whole, including scratching posts, feeding grounds, dens and scent-marking spots. This would mean that the new cat would inherit the same routes and routines as the old cat, providing fresh sightings over the years in the same area, often in the same spot.

Another possibility is that the last cub an old female produces, learns the hunting and home territory from its parent and later takes it over when its mother dies.

Unfortunately behaviour patterns cannot be determined

until the animals are studied in their natural conditions. Even a captured specimen in a zoo cage only shows the external appearance of the creature, not its natural behaviour pattern.

If some of the Black Dogs of folklore are the same as the mystery cats of the twentieth century, then the animals have been with us for centuries, possibly thousands of years. Perhaps a very intelligent feline species long ago watched man's destruction of its relatives and learnt an important lesson. The apparently weak hairless ape was very dangerous when crossed. As more and more species were destroyed by this modern upstart, then the intelligent cat might have understood that its survival depended on keeping out of man's way and not directly challenging him in any form, either as a direct attack or as a rival to the food chain.

In this modern age of technology a chance encounter with a big cat no longer produces superstitious fear in man, only curiosity. Perhaps the cat's main defence has finally been destroyed, but fortunately at a time in the evolution of the man beast when it is learning to be tolerant of other creatures, perhaps even regretting the destruction it has caused in the past.

As world opinion gradually unites against the hunting of the whales, the destruction of the elephants and the wearing of murdered fur, it is perhaps the right time for the mystery animal to reveal itself so that it can be granted protection.

It is now up to the scientists and the authorities to combine forces and attempt to discover the truth.

Do the animals exist?

The amount of the evidence collected certainly suggests they do.

What are the animals?

Only the capture of specimens can answer this question. Only then can the question of protection be considered.

This leaves us with perhaps the most crucial question of all – how, when so much has been tried and failed, such enormous resources and manpower have been pitted against the animals without success, can the creatures be identified?

10

Mystery Skulls and Missing Bodies

One fact constantly quoted by sceptics when attempting to disprove that anything other than the odd rogue dog was roving the moors is the obvious lack of a body. Surely, they argue, if there are genuine big cats roaming the countryside, then they have to die of natural causes. Discounting people who occasionally claim to have killed a big cat, a great many of the mystery felines reported over the last twenty years should have died of disease or old age. Yet, for all the intensive searches in the areas where the beasts are claimed to be, no large feline corpses have been discovered.

The behaviour of those claiming to have killed a big cat is also hard to understand, if they are telling the truth. Why has no one called in the authorities when suddenly confronted with a large feline that obviously represented a danger to farm stock and the public? Why did these people imagine they would be prosecuted rather than applauded for disposing of an obviously dangerous predator?

When Alex Pollock, MP, approached the Scottish Office Minister for Home Affairs, Michael Ancram, to inquire about protection for exotic feral cats, he was told:

Until such time as the animal is scientifically identified, I cannot say what statutory provisions might apply and there is no form of interim protection order which could be made in advance of identification. Should the animal prove to be a large domestic or feral cat it would be protected in the same way as other domestic animals, under the provisions of the Protection of Animals (Scotland) Act 1912. If however it is found to be a species of wildcat which is one of the animals listed in Schedule 6 of the Wildlife and Countryside Act 1981, certain methods of killing or taking it would be prohibited. In the event of it being identified as an escaped or released panther then I am afraid I have no powers to issue a protection order which could prevent it from being shot or killed in some other way.

Such a statement from a government minister reveals the uncomfortable truth. If the various panther, puma or lion sightings are genuine, whether they were of released or escaped big cats, then the only restraints on any member of the general public taking pot-shots at the unfortunate animals are the normal firearms restrictions imposed on anyone using a gun. The implications are horrendous. Any of the big cat species at large in the British countryside is at the mercy of any finger on a legal trigger.

The chances of an ordinary marksman killing a big cat is remote. Even experienced hunters admit that a big cat is the most difficult of all animals to kill. The cat is extremely muscular, making it difficult to hit the animal in a vital organ. It is also quick in its movements. A running cat weaves its body in a fluid rippling motion which constantly alters the shape of the target, making it difficult to get a clear shot at a vulnerable spot. The risk of wounding rather than killing the hunted animal is high. If the idea of a number of leopards or pumas or other big cats roaming the countryside is disturbing, the thought of a wounded big cat at large is terrifying.

So, despite the fact that shooting one would not be breaking the law, still the rumours persist of people having shot a large cat and immediately disposing of the body for fear of prosecution. Clearly some stories are just hoaxes, or myths, like the man who claimed to have shot a bear and buried the carcase on Molland Common. Others have a definite ring of truth, the witnesses sounding sincere and embarrassed about their actions.

Strangely enough, those responsible for killing a smaller animal seem to be quite willing to come forward and explain their involvement. When a leopard cat was shot by a farmer near Widecombe on Dartmoor in April 1988, the body was immediately handed over to the authorities for identification. In February the following year, when farmer Norman Evans found the carcase of a jungle cat close to his home near Ludlow in Shropshire, he reported his finding and the body was handed over to scientists who thought it had died from injuries, possibly inflicted by a car. Another jungle cat was killed in Hampshire and two escaped leopard cats have been killed in recent years in the Scottish borders. All were immediately reported to the police.

These two species are not much larger than a domestic cat. Still, they excited enough curiosity for the finders to report their discoveries. Frequently witnesses claiming to have killed puma- or leopard-size cats, or to have discovered their carcases, not only remain silent about them, they don't even photograph the animals out of curiosity, to try to identify them at a later date. The immediate reaction is to cast doubt on the validity of such stories.

In 1982 Mrs Gionna Prew discovered a brown cat the size of a Labrador dog lying dead on a roadside verge near Wargrave in Berkshire. A vet who examined the animal confirmed it to be a labrador-size cat, similar to a puma. Still no one thought to report the find to the authorities. The body was buried in an orchard at the rear of the house, but unfortunately predators had raided the grave before my attempt to dig it up. I found only bone fragments and some ginger hairs, nothing that could be identified.

In 1984 a Welsh hill farmer claimed to have trapped a big

cat on his land and then to have thrown the carcase into the nearby river. He said he was not 'having conservationists telling me what to do on my own land'. He described the animal as having a short tail. For two years researchers had been monitoring sightings in that area of a puma-size cat with a noticeably short tail. Following the story of the dead cat being discovered, no sighting of the short-tailed cat has been recorded. Coincidence? Perhaps, but certainly back-up circumstantial evidence that a short-tailed big cat did indeed meet its end on the farmer's hillside in Wales.

The reticence to come forward is puzzling, except perhaps where poaching on private property is involved. But even then it is odd that curiosity is not enough to persuade those responsible to disguise the circumstances in which the carcase is obtained. It would be a simple enough matter, after all, to remove the carcase from private land, shove it into the boot of a car and dump it on a suitable public site before announcing the discovery. Even when there is illegal use of a gun or trap involved, anyone could claim to have stumbled over the already dead body while on an innocent country ramble.

Because smaller exotic cats continue to be reported, if found or killed, while the big ones are ignored or hidden away, the immediate assumption is that all the claims for big cats apparently living wild in Britain are treated as hoaxes or figments of fertile imaginations. There are, however, two notable exceptions – the Cannich puma, trapped by Ted Noble on the hillside at the bottom of Miss Jessie Chisholm's garden, and a skull found on Dartmoor, just a few miles from the hunting-ground of the Exmoor beast.

In 1988 sixteen-year-old Simon Hopwood and his friend, Sebastian Carnell, were walking along a lane near the village of Lustleigh, about five miles from the Devon market-town of Newton Abbot, when they spotted the white dome of a skull lying in the long tangled grass on the far side of the hedge. Most people wouldn't have given the skull a second glance. Animal skeletons, especially those of sheep, litter the moorlands, and are often to be found along the road verges where the animals have been hit by cars and their bones picked clean by scavangers. Often only the skull, the least appetising part of the carcase, remains. Simon was a wildlife enthusiast who had a large collection of animal skulls, and so the two boys scrambled over to retrieve the half-hidden bone. Judging by its size, they expected it to be the remains of a pony or a calf. When Simon lifted it up and brushed off the moss and other debris, he realised immediately that he was holding the skull of a large feline.

Naturally excited, the two boys searched around for other bones. They found both sections of the lower jaw, complete with most of the teeth. Then they took the remains home and reported their unusual find. The local paper carried the news item, naming the skull as that of a puma. There the story might have ended if Professor Charles Thomas, who lived in Cornwall, had not spotted the report and sent a copy of it to me. Professor Thomas was taking a personal interest in the search for the mystery big cats, having seen one himself near Okehampton when he was a boy. I contacted Simon and he allowed me to borrow the mystery skull for a year in an attempt to get it identified.

On examination, it was obvious at once that the skull did not belong to a puma or any feline of medium-size. It was far too large, and was more in the size range of a young lion. It was definitely feline in appearance, with extremely large canine teeth, the upper ones extending so far that the teeth would have protruded well below the lip when the animal's mouth was closed. The lower canines were almost equal in length to the upper ones, whereas in most big cat species the lower canines are usually considerably shorter than the upper teeth. Despite these huge fangs, the space for the lower incisors was extremely narrow. Most of the incisors were missing, just two remaining in the upper jaw and none in the lower jaw. The size of the root sockets suggested a variation in the size of the lower teeth, the two central spaces being slightly smaller than those next to them and the two outer sockets a fraction of the size of the inner ones.

Although the dentition of the skull is striking, it is possible that the animal simply had a deformed mouth, perhaps due to being reared in captivity on an unhealthy diet that caused it to grow misshapen teeth. However, if the dentition of this particular animal was deformed, could another totally unrelated animal have an almost identical bite?

In the spring of 1988 a farm in the North-east Highlands of Scotland, near the town of Keith, was losing ewes and lambs to an unseen predator. One carcase was left behind and a local veterinary surgeon, Neil Sargison, performed a post-mortem examination on the dead lamb, a 12b three-day-old greyface. He found that the lamb's head was missing, having been torn off at the atlanto-occipital joint. This had occurred after death and would have required considerable force. There were two sets of puncture-marks in the skin on either side of the ribcage, each pair of marks being spaced about 3½ inches apart. There was extensive brusing associated with each wound. All the wounds penetrated the ribcage, the second rib on the right side was broken and the seventh to ninth ribs shattered. The right humerus was broken and the left shoulder dislocated.

Neil Sargison concluded that the lamb had died as a result of being gripped and bitten over the ribcage. He found that none of the other injuries had severe bruising associated with them and so must have occurred after the animal's death. He commented, 'These findings do not match anything that I have seen as a result of fox or dog worrying.'

A few days later he examined a live lamb from the same farm that had survived an attack. The lamb had similar injuries over its ribcage and had been very lucky to escape death. A second lamb had vanished without trace.

I attended the post-mortem on the dead lamb, having with me the feline skull found by the boys on Dartmoor. During the examination, I inserted the canines of the skull into the injuries on the carcase, simulating a bite across the back, copying what appeared to be the position of the grip that the predator had used to kill the lamb. The huge canines of the Dartmoor skull slid neatly into the puncture wounds without any sort of manipulation. Whatever had killed the lamb in the Scottish Highlands had an almost identical bite pattern as that of the Dartmoor mystery cat!

If the Dartmoor cat was simply a known species of big cat with deformed dentition, then it would appear that it had a twin across the border in the far north-east of Scotland.

So where did the skull come from? Well, the obvious conclusion is that the unfortunate creature died in the wild, possibly – as it was found so close to a road – as a result of an unreported collision with a car. The rest of the carcase would have rotted and been dispersed by other predators, so that only the skull remained to be found by Simon and Sebastian. Another equally plausible theory is that the skull was tossed out of the window of a passing car, either in order to dispose of it or in the hope, as an amusing hoax, it would be discovered. A third theory was that it had never actually lain in its moorland grave but had simply been obtained by the boys themselves as an elaborate hoax.

Obviously the origin and identification of the skull is important, for if a known species of exotic big cat did live wild in the area for any length of time, its presence could account for some of the reported sightings of mystery felines, and it would almost certainly have been the culprit for some of the sheep killed and eaten on the moors. A feral large black leopard wandering around Devon would explain the witness reports of large black panther-like cats and would also satisfy the scientist's argument that, if a genuine big cat was on the loose, it was of a known species. If the animal had been a lioness, then it could explain the sightings of brown big cats, and even perhaps the dark coloured felines, for the shadowy figure of a brown animal seen in poor light could appear to be black.

The discovery of the existence of a feral exotic big cat of either of these species would prove that witnesses had indeed seen large felines wandering around the Devon countryside, and the solution of the mystery would be welcomed by the scientists as a perfectly acceptable conclusion to the mystery. However, if the skull is that of a tiger or of a male lion, it can have no connection with the reported sightings because no witness had claimed to have seen the distinctive striped or maned big cats. The identification of the skull as that of a male lion or tiger, or proof that it had been thrown away, or else placed there as a joke or a hoax, makes it of no further interest to anyone.

If the find is genuine, and it cannot be easily identified as the skull of a known species, then it opens up all sorts of exciting possibilities. Identification of the skull is crucial, either in an attempt to solve at least the mystery predator of Devon and identify the Exmoor beast, or to eliminate it from the enquiries. With no financial backing to enable me to travel round the world, visiting the various experts in person, I had a series of photographs taken and, together with measurements, sent these off to a number of renowned zoologists who were willing to examine the skull.

The results were far from conclusive. After Jerry Herman and Dr Andrew Kitchener of the Royal Museum of Scotland examined the photographs and compared them with various specimens in the museum collection, they both offered the opinion that the skull was that of a leopard. Herman did comment that, 'Of course photographs are no substitute for seeing the actual skull and comparing it with specimens in the collection.'

Dr Colin P. Groves of the National University of Canberra, Australia, and a member of the International Society of Cryptozoology, was of a different opinion. He suggested the skull was that of a sub-adult lion. He considered that the lowness of the sagittal crest, widely open sutures and long (unworn) canines suggested the animal had not been mature, although he felt he needed to examine the basilar suture to be sure. He felt the size of the skull, length 11 inches (about 280mm), made it too big for anything among living cats but a lion or a tiger. At the same time, it was smaller than adults of these two species (except, perhaps, for the small Indonesian tigers). He noted that the morphology of the region around the infraorbital foramen and the shape of the malar-maxillary suture, was typically pantherine. He considered that if the skull was accepted as *Panthera*, then the characteristics that made it a lion rather than a tiger were the form of the interorbital region (both from the side and from in front), the posterior margin of the nasals and what he could see of the mandible and carnassial teeth. He commented that leopards are more similar to lions than to tigers, but it would have been a truly enormous (not impossible) leopard. The carnassial did not appear to be at all right.

Dr Frank Turk of Exeter University favoured a small, fairly young, but adult tiger when he examined the photographs. He pointed out that the photographs do not show many of the features which would have been helpful to see but, he suggested, everything he could see fitted a tiger and no other big cat. He compared it with the skull of a leopard which he had, and with many drawings and descriptions of the skulls of lion, jaguar, puma and other more unlikely candidates. He found the Dartmoor skull differed very significantly from them all.

Other opinions simply echoed the confusion, leopards, young lions and young tigers all being suggested. What should be made of this? Obviously identification of the Dartmoor skull is not a simple matter and the fact that it had to be attempted in a number of cases by means of measurements and photographs did not make the task any easier. Some zoologists were able to examine the skull itself, though this did not help to lessen the confusion over identification.

At the time of writing, there the matter rests. It is to be hoped that new research, involving genetic identification from bone samples, will eventually settle the dispute as to whether the creature was in fact, lion, tiger, leopard or something else.

Another fruitful line of research would be the modelling of facial tissue on to the skull to find out what the animal actually looked like. This method has been used successfully in a number of police cases in which a skull has been obtained but no other means of identification. Scientists can build up the skull by careful reconstruction of tissue and muscle in clay, using a very detailed scale of depth. The results have produced amazing likenesses of victims that have been recognised by friends and relatives.

The method has also been used for the archaeological reconstruction of prehistoric heads, providing us with a glimpse of Neanderthal or Cro-Magnon man. Some details, such as hair type, style or colour, cannot be assessed from the bare bones, but even those can sometimes be guessed by remnants of hair attached to the skull. Obviously, in the case of the Dartmoor cat, type and position of ears and colour of coat can never be estimated, but the actual shape of nose and jowls can help identify the species. A lion, a tiger and a leopard each have different facial shapes. The tiger is broad and square-muzzled, the lion leaner, the leopard smaller and shorter-jawed.

If the Devonshire skull belongs to any of these three suggested species, then even without ears and coat colour, it should be possible to identify it. On the other hand, if it does not resemble any of the known three species, then it would be interesting to compare the reconstructed cat's appearance with descriptions provided by witnesses.

11

From Cornwall to Caithness

The fear of the South Molton police that one day the circus could begin all over again is not unfounded. Ever since the police were faced with the impossible task of protecting farmers' sheep from the ravages of the Exmoor beast, other hunts and other beasts have been reported throughout the British Isles. From Cornwall to Caithness witnesses today are reporting sightings of leopard-size unidentified cats roaming the countryside and hundreds of farmers are still finding their sheep slaughtered and eaten. Yet the media no longer treats the cat hunts with the intensity it once gave to the Surrey puma or the Exmoor beast. It is simply no longer a novelty. What is new in the situation is the number of witnesses reporting their sightings and the degree to which these are being taken seriously. It is also new for farmers to examine dead sheep closely to determine how they died. Representatives of the National Farmer's Union and staff at the Ministry of Agriculture are trying to study the situation as a whole and their findings are frightening. Sheep losses to unknown predators are increasing and large numbers of sheep simply vanish without trace from their British fields.

The farmers and the Ministry of Agriculture cannot balance the books.

Sheep have always wandered off and become lost or have been stolen, and both still account for some of the missing ewes, but not all. Sheep are killed by dogs and die of other causes to be devoured by nature's scavengers, but again these do not explain the enormous unaccountable losses across the countryside.

In April 1983, while Sergeant Goodman was trying to track down the mystery predator of Exmoor, armed police were using a helicopter to hunt for a brown cat spotted near the village of Stokenchurch in Buckinghamshire. The animal was seen by Philip Viccars from his garden near the village school. 'I thought it was a peculiar-looking dog,' he said. 'I went up the garden to get a closer look and saw it was feline and slender in appearance, with a very long thick tail, small head and short legs. It was about the size of an Alsatian and was coloured deep fawn with merging black spots.' He called his wife and sister to see the animal and, together with their neighbour Margaret Brooks, they watched it through binoculars for about half an hour. Six policemen with a tracker-dog searched the area, no doubt persuaded to take the sighting seriously by the fact that the country had been the scene of various cat sightings over the years, including one by two policemen at Stoke Poges in 1964.

In the following month, while marine commandos were huddled in dripping hides around South Molton, police were touring the Cuffley area in Hertfordshire with loudhailers, calling on local residents to stay out of their gardens while a search was carried out for a lion-like animal that had been reported by several witnesses, including a policeman on patrol.

During November of the same year, Cortingham and Grays police stations in Essex were receiving reports of a black panther-like beast on the prowl in the vicinity of Bulphan and Hordon-on-the-Hill. An armed search was made for the creature.

Sightings received less publicity in 1984, but in August of that year mounted police officers and armed farmers in Lancashire searched the Rossendale Valley for a cat as big as a lioness which was thought to have killed and eaten sheep in the hills above Bacup, after 14-year-old Owen Jepson spotted a puma-size cat while walking across Swineshaw Moor. He said, 'It was 4.30 in the afternoon, a bright sunny day. Suddenly, only about eighty yards away I saw a great pair of hind legs, paws and a tail about two and a half feet long, leaping through a clump of rushes. The creature was beige-coloured. I picked up a stick and gave chase.'

The animal made good its escape but local farmer Geoff Dootson found a dead sheep nearby that he described as having 'a wound like a dinner-plate and its ribs were crushed.' Near the carcase he found paw prints which, he said, had four circular marks the size of golf balls.

In October 1985 armed police searched the Harrogate area after they received reports of a sighting of a panther-like animal. The owners of Knaresborough Zoo and Flamingo Park Zoo confirmed that their big cats were still safely in their cages. A veterinary surgeon with a tranquilliser was on hand while officers checked the Bilton Hall Lane area. Mrs Pool, a mother of four, told the *Yorkshire Post* that the people who saw the creature later were country folk. 'They know a dog or a fox when they see one. This thing was certainly not a dog or a fox.'

The following month farmer Geoffrey Fisher disturbed a large cat on his land in the Forest of Dean near Westbury-on-Severn. He was walking his Alsatian dog when they encountered the creature. It reared up to attack the dog, which promptly backed off, terrified. Mr Fisher said, 'That's what shocked me, as it was unlike Leya to be put off in that way. She took after the animal which was near some of my sheep. Then suddenly she veered off the attack and went around in a broad circle. I thought it was a black Labrador at first, but it was a large, jet black cat. It loped off at an amazing speed.'

Sightings were recorded over a number of years, of a similar animal on the outskirts of Kings Forest at Eleveden in Suffolk. Police and gamekeepers unsuccessfully attempted to trap the animal on a number of occasions.

In 1986 the Durham police were searching for a large black pantherlike animal seen by a number of witnesses. Sheep had been killed and eaten in the Trimdon area, where most of the sightings had been reported. In September the sightings increased dramatically. Brian Rothery of Ferryhill was out walking his Dobermann dog when he saw the animal apparently stalking some children who were playing around the old colliery buildings. 'I saw this black thing and at first I thought it was a small horse, then I realised it was too long to be a horse. It was standing with its head down towards the grass. It was a large, long black cat, bigger than my Dobermann.' The children became aware that the animal was watching them and the cat made off at speed. A few days earlier a motorist had spotted an Alsatian dog-size black cat loping across a field near Thinford Crossroads, with a smaller black animal at its side. In the same area the driver of a parked lorry was terrified when a large black cat leapt on to his bonnet and snarled at him through the windscreen. He called for assistance on his CB radio, but the cat made off when it was caught in the headlights of an approaching car. On 28th of that month, a motorist driving near Bowburn, the scene of sightings earlier in the year, saw a black cat about four feet long and two feet high carrying a rabbit in its mouth. A police spokesman said that it was vital the animal was located as all the witnesses appeared positive the creature was a big cat.

Durham City policeman Eddie Bell became so intrigued by the continual sightings that he began a personal study of the reports. In May 1988 AA-man Colin Crook was driving his van when he caught sight of a large grey cat in his headlights at the junction of the A68 with the A6082. He said, 'I was returning home after work. It was in my headlights and was quite obviously some kind of big cat. It was the strangest animal I've ever seen.' He said it was about four feet long, had a flat face and walked with the ease of a cat. It stared at him and then walked off into the nearby field. He noted it had a limp. In September 1990 a tethered mare was found dead at Spennymoor after a coal-depot security officer reported seeing an Alsatian-size animal attacking the horse. The mare had large bites to the chest, and had strangled itself in its efforts to break free. The following day a large black panther-size cat was seen by gypsies nearby. Despite constant searches, the Durham police found nothing.

In April 1988 witnesses, including a policeman, reported a black panther at Burgess Hill in East Sussex. Sussex had been the scene of a number of big cat sightings during the 1960s and 1970s.

During August that year experts from London Zoo were standing by, ready to move in to sedate a pumalike cat seen in North London. It was reported to have killed domestic pets and wild animals around the suburban gardens of Edgware. A police spokesman said, 'We are treating this matter seriously. We don't know what it is but we are treating it as a dangerous animal.' Mrs Susie Hopkins found the creature in her garden, where it killed her kitten Pansy. She described how she heard the kitten screaming outside late one night. 'My husband and I opened the back door and there was this huge greyish beast, ready to pounce. It bit Pansy's neck and she died immediately. Then it bounded off, crashing through the undergrowth of the school next to us.'

Another resident in the area also encountered a big cat in his garden in the same month. Tony Finn glimpsed two glowing yellow eyes in his car headlights as he pulled into his drive late at night. He called his friend, Adrian Slowey, and together they searched the garden with a flashlight. Suddenly a huge black cat reared up in front of them and bounded off. Tony Finn said, 'Its face was the size of a steering-wheel. I like cats – but not that big.' Mrs Margaret Corbel saw the beast one morning. She looked out of her window to see a huge cat crouched on the branch of a tree. 'I couldn't believe my eyes. It was black and tan and staring at me.' She called her husband, who saw the creature before it jumped down out of the tree and ran off. The animal became known as the Edgware Tiger and vanished as mysteriously as it had arrived. Its identity was never established.

Armed police and farmers were searching the Derbyshire countryside for a black panther-like animal during November the following year. Steve Monaghan of New Mills said, 'I first saw the thing in April but I don't think anyone believed me.' When he spotted the big cat again in November he called the police. Police Sergeant Phil Lucic arrived and confirmed the farmer's sighting. He said, 'It was not a stray dog. It was big, black and catlike. It was a hundred and fifty yards away and we watched it through binoculars for twenty minutes.' He called for assistance, but when his armed colleagues arrived, the cat had vanished. A police officer, no doubt inspired by Sergeant Lucic's report, said 'We are treating this seriously. We are warning hikers to stay away. They should take no chances.' The police also stated publicly that they had been advised there was no choice but to kill the animal. 'Putting a transquilliser dart in it would mean the marksman had to be at the most twenty yards away and it would be five minutes before it took effect. Setting traps would be expensive and complicated and there is no guarantee they would work.'

Such a statement in 1989, six years after the hunt for the beast of Exmoor, suggests that the Derbyshire police had attempted to research their subject and learn from the failures of others. In April 1992 an elderly woman, Mrs Kathleen Topcliff, disturbed a panther-size black cat actually inside her house at Hayfield on the edge of the moors. She tried to chase it outside and received a bite on the hand, needing two stitches, before the animal made its escape through an open window. Inspector Rick Laithwaite of the Gossop police said, 'We have had repeated sightings but this is the first time anyone has seen it so close.'

In May 1988 PC Ian Harvey of West Malling police, in Kent, reported seeing a large knee-high, rusty-coloured cat walking along the Pilgrim's Way, at Trottiscliffe, near West Malling. In May the following year, safari park staff were consulted in an attempt to trap big cats seen in the Kidderminster, Hereford and Worcester areas after a number of sightings of puma-size felines.

Retired company director Douglas South and his wife Joyce have recorded two sightings of a mystery catlike animal in Devon. The first, according to a report in the *Western Morning News*, was in February 1989 when the couple watched a black catlike animal run at great speed down a field; the second was on the evening of 25th May when 'it was in vision for at least thirty seconds and we had a very close look'. The creature was creeping along the wall at the rear of their property. It 'was black, about eighteen inches tall and about three feet long, with a disproportionately small head. It had a long tail with thick hind quarters and thick large paws, and it was heavily scarred on its hind quarters. 'I am not given to being scared,' Mr South said, 'but it was a frightening beast.' His description was similar to the beast sighted not long before at Cullompton by a police officer, M.C.P. James, although the animal he had watched as it ran across a motorway slip road had been reddish brown in colour.

Following years of sightings of big cats throughout Wales, I photographed a black panther-size cat (opposite page 55) which I saw running with a grey striped cub at Tonmawr, near Neath in 1982. Despite numerous reports of other big cat sightings received by the police, the animals were never caught. Three years later Mrs Susan Howells was riding near her parents' farm at Kenfig Hill, Mid-Glamorgan, when she encountered a huge savage-looking fawn cat the size of a lion. 'It was definitely a big cat. My horse was terrified, shaking with fright, and nearly bolted.' A Forestry Commission official confirmed that plaster casts of large cat prints had been taken from the area. The police stated 'We are obviously concerned about people's safety. We have searched the area but it is an impossible task.'

Five years later two other riders confronted a huge lion-size cat, this time in Margram Forest. Mrs Anne Phillips and her daughter Lorna were near the edge of the forest when they spotted the animal. 'At first I thought it was a Great Dane or a Labrador and then as we rode closer it seemed to get much bigger,' she said. 'I thought it had escaped from a zoo. It came out of the trees and down the side of an embankment. It was moving with a spring-like action from its back legs. When we got up close, it just seemed to fly away, it was moving so fast.'

Scotland has produced big cat sightings for years. In 1927 an article appeared in the *Daily Express* of 14th January under the headline: 'Mystery Tiger of the North'.

Sheep and goats were attacked in the wild mountain districts of Inverness-shire and traps were set to catch 'the mysterious marauder'. Tracks like those of a gigantic cat were found in the soft mud of the moorland bogs.

Shepherds reported having seen an animal 'like a leopard but without spots on its coat, stalking the sheep'.

The article continued to report on three brown lynx-like animals being killed in Scotland. Their origins were a mystery.

During the 1970s and 1980s brown and black leopard-like cats were being reported across the Highlands. Over a period of years Miss Jessie Chisholm constantly contacted the Inverness police because she was seeing leopard-size cats in the forest around her isolated cottage at Cannich, outside Inverness. Some she described as black, like panthers, others brown, like pumas, and at least one animal as golden-coated with dark thin stripes. At first the police did not take Miss Chisholm's reports seriously, despite other witnesses' claims to seeing big cats in the same area. Finally, with the help of a neighbouring farmer, Ted Noble, Miss Chisholm built a trap at the forest edge and caught an adult puma. The mystery of the Cannich cat sightings should have been solved by the capture of the big cat, but instead the situation was complicated because Miss Chisholm, Ted Noble, and other local witnesses declared that the puma did not resemble the mystery cats they had seen before. The puma, an elderly female, was tame and obviously had been released at some time from captivity. The evidence suggested she had been feral in the Cannich area for about two years. After her capture, local residents still reported sightings of other big cats with different coat colour variations.

After the capture of the Cannich puma, the media has never given the same attention to the Scottish reports that they have to those in England, possibly because the wilderness of the Highlands destroys the fantasy of big cats roaming undetected. With its great stretches of forest filled with wild deer and the vast moorlands grazed by semi-wild sheep, rabbits and hares, the Highlands of Scotland would seem an ideal home for any number of exotic feral cats.

The *Forres Gazette*, covering the Morayshire farming area, reported a number of sightings of large black cats in 1884. In February of that year a woman walking her two Labrador dogs in the woodland at the edge of Monaughty Forest disturbed a huge black cat that was eating a deer carcase. She said, 'It was a terrifying experience, I've been walking in the area for fifteen years and never seen anything like that – it's something I'd never want to repeat. I was aware of something not far from the track and, as I looked, it turned its head towards me. It was feeding. I've never seen anything like it. The dogs are a big breed of Labrador and nothing normally upsets them – whatever that was in the wood did though. The dog stopped mid-track just as though cement had been poured over him. The animal was certainly bigger than the dogs, had a shining black coat and what appeared to be a long sweeping tail. It was longer than my dog and to me looked more like a panther than a puma.'

A week later a jogger reported seeing a large black animal

bounding out of a field and into a wood on the outskirts of the town of Forres. By May there had been a number of sightings recorded in the area. In June three golfers spotted a mystery animal on the edge of the golf course. Dennis McLeod said his friend John Main first noticed the beast. 'He asked me what was lying in the trees just opposite. I told him it looked like a log but then the log moved.' He described the animal as black, the size of a Labrador dog. 'It certainly was not a dog. We got a good enough look at it to realise that. There appeared to be a ruff round its thick neck, almost as if its hackles were raised, but it made no noise and just seemed to stare at us.'

By the spring of 1985 there had been so many reported sightings of panther-size cats in the Morayshire area that, on April 24th, the Member of Parliament, Alex Pollock, was reported to have approached the Scottish Office Minister for Home Affairs to inquire about protection for the big cat in the Morayshire area. Mr Pollock commented, 'This was a very unusual inquiry but one which I felt it proper to make in view of the intense local interest in this matter. Given that no positive conclusions have yet been reached about the nature and origin of the creature it seemed worth while exploring whether anything could be done to protect it until the mystery is resolved.'

Morayshire was not the only part of Scotland where big cats were being seen and farmstock killed and eaten. During the winter of 1984, Knapdale farmers in Argyllshire were hoping tracks in the snow would lead them to the lair of a puma-like animal that was killing sheep on local farms. In September the following year black and brown puma-size cats were reported prowling around a large building site on the outskirts of Inverness. Mr Gordon Schmitz, site agent for Hugh MacRae, the company building the houses on the new estate, admitted he had seen the animals several times. He said, 'One was bigger than an Alsatian dog with a long curled tail. It was black or very dark. When the boys were stripping top soil off the site, we saw it two or three days in succession. Three or four of us standing together saw it on more than one occasion.' The Inverness cats certainly weren't the same animal as the one seen in the Forres area for it was still being sighted during the autumn of that year.

One employee of a Scottish newspaper was able to provide a firsthand account of the mystery big cats. In November 1986 Tom Robertson, a printer with the Aberdeen-based *Press and Journal*, was driving home from work along the B9119 road at 4 a.m. when he saw what he described as 'a huge, jet black cat with a long tail'. In 1988 police began to receive sightings of big black cats seen in the Banffshire area, including the grounds of historic Duff House. By June 1991 Aberdeen police were hunting for a black panther-like beast reported in their area after a number of sightings around Hatton of Fintray. A horse was attacked in its stable, bolting through a barbed wire fence to escape. A police spokesman said, 'We have no idea what or where this creature is but it is no West Highland Terrier. It is big and must be caught. This beast is very large, bigger than any Alsatian and obviously vicious.'

If the police and Ministry of Agriculture are beginning to come to terms with the existence of unidentified cats living in the British countryside, the residents in areas where cats are reported to have been seen are also coming to accept the existence of the cats as part of the countryside fauna. Farmers and gamekeepers who have seen the animals need no proof that they are there. Preventing attacks on their stock has proved a dispiriting failure and the overall cost of sheep losses is high. Individually farmers cannot afford to take the right measures against the cats, and even with all the skill of highly trained men and equipment brought to bear, the marauders seem able to avoid anything pitted against them, as the events on Exmoor showed all too clearly.

Only a complete understanding of the species and its behaviour can give the hunters any chance of success, and this information can be discovered only by all the various bodies getting together, and pooling their knowledge, skills and equipment in a combined action. If the police and the marines had been given the knowledge at the beginning of the Exmoor hunt that they had acquired by the end of it, they might have succeeded in ending the career of the predator that is still dining off the South Molton lambs.

To trap or kill an animal, one has to know what it is and understand its behaviour. To date, the beasts have always been put on the alert by the increased activity around them. A farmer finds his sheep killed and eaten and, deciding to deal with the predator, believing it to be dogs or foxes, he starts patrolling his fields at night. The attacks continue, despite his efforts, and friends and neighbours join him in the hunt. Perhaps publicity produces reports of catlike beasts seen around the killing site. Frightened or angry, the farmers call in the police, who in their turn, search the area.

All this activity warns the predator that it is in danger. It continues its night time attacks but behaves with extra caution. It never kills to a pattern, never returns to a kill, and will never take poisoned carrion or live bait when it has to walk through prey to reach it. Because of this, it cannot be tempted into a trap or ambush.

Unless the entire hunting territory is cleared of all natural food, including rabbits, deer, sheep and even birds, the predator is not going to bother with any food, alive or dead, that is found in suspicious circumstances. With its sense of smell and acute hearing, it is well aware of any hunters around, long before the hunters are aware of it.

So how can these creatures ever be caught? Unless killed in a road traffic accident, the first specimen will almost certainly be shot. Enticing the animal into the range of a marksman, as occurred, even though the results were unsuccessful on Exmoor will be far easier than persuading it to enter a trap. Although I do not approve of killing an animal just to prove it exists, I have no conscience about the shooting of a known sheep-killer, not just because of the financial loss to the farmers, but for the protection of the sheep, live animals have been found with their legs torn off, or the guts trailing from their ripped bellies, and such attacks must be prevented if possible.

If everything tried so far has met with failure, what then should be done?

There should be an investigative government body set up, connected to the Ministry of Agriculture, so that when a farmer first discovers he is losing sheep in suspicious circumstances he has someone to contact. Otherwise he should do nothing except go about his normal day routine. If the attacks persist, then the immediate area should be cleared of almost all sheep, the Ministry of Agriculture making provision for the temporary accommodation of evacuated flocks, perhaps using set aside land on other farms. A small flock of sheep should be left grazing in the area where the attacks have occurred, preferably old broken-mouthed animals without lambs. Basically this scheme is aimed at providing the predator with a supply of free meals without too much disturbance and at a minimum of financial cost. Animal lovers will shudder at the idea of sheep being used as target animals, but it has to be understood that sheep will die anyway. Surely it is better that old animals at the end of their lives should be preyed upon, rather than young breeding ewes with lambs at foot? Examination of carcases reveals that the death of the victim is normally instantaneous, only the occasional target being fleet of foot and alert enough to attempt an escape, resulting often in terrible mutilation. An older slower animal has less chance of becoming an untidy kill.

With the attacker having been lulled into a false sense of security, a hide should be built and then left unused for the predator to become accustomed to the new structure. After the pattern of kills is clearly established, only then should a professional marksman slip quietly into the hide when the next kill is expected.

There can still be no guarantee of success, but the chances of failure will have been lessened.

It will be far more difficult to capture an animal alive. Nevertheless I believe it can be done, employing the same technique but using a marksman with a tranquilliser dart fitted with a tiny transmitter so that the animal can be traced once it has dropped.

This will all cost money, but perhaps less than the disorganised searches across the countryside that have yielded nothing, certainly less than the enormous sheep losses suffered by farmers. Government funding has to be made available for the protection of the farmer's livestock, if not for the identification of the predators. The alternative – of allowing individual farmers and local guns to take the law into their own hands – is a recipe for disaster. What could be more worrying than the thought of an amateur shot injuring a hunting big cat, whatever its species? That is how man killers are created.

12

Confounding the Experts

Nine years after Andy Wilkins had led the marines across the muddy fields and moorlands of Exmoor, I returned to South Molton to interview witnesses and to bring myself up-to-date. A new hunt was in progress just a few miles away across the border on the Cornish moors. The 'Beast of Bodmin' was causing a small flurry of interest, but a couple of local TV crews and a few wandering reporters could not compare with the heady days of the media circus of 1983.

Among the hunters attracted to the region was John Henry Lambert, who preferred to be known as Tracker. He was a likable, eccentric wanderer, living the image of Rambo and Davy Crocket combined, claiming American Indian and gypsy ancestry. He left Bodmin to travel to the tragic war zone of Croatia, where just weeks later, on 20th July, he was struck by a bullet and fatally wounded while helping to transport the injured to hospital at Turic, dying six days later at the age of 35.

Like most other rural areas of Britain, Cornwall has been the source of a number of big cat sightings over the years. In June 1973 Dave Nicholas was walking with a companion through Tehidy Woods, near Camborne, when they spotted a puma-like animal sauntering along the path ahead of them. Walter Berry of Penhalvean saw a black leopard-size cat near Stithians Reservoir in 1980, and twice John Cockle spotted a sandy brown puma-size cat near his home at Truro.

Unlike in Scotland or in Surrey, the Cornish sightings have trickled in slowly, many people believing that the Exmoor animal simply extended its hunting territory from time to time, perhaps when its home ground became too crowded with bounty hunters and *Daily Express* readers.

A dark puma-size cat was reported in 1992, at Bolventor on Bodmin Moor, just three miles from the famed tourist spot, Jamaica Inn. Local farmers complained of losing sheep to an unknown and powerful predator. Mrs Rosemary Rhodes of Ninestones Farm was certain that her lambs were being killed by a big cat. One of her employees, Don Rogers, and his son were out checking the flock at night when they found themselves face to face with a large dark grey or brown catlike animal as they swung the beam from a powerful torch across a field.

'It stopped dead in the light and stared at me for a minute, its eyes reflecting back yellow,' Mr Rogers told me. 'I've been born and bred on the moor and I know what animals look like up here, I know the deer and sheep's eyes and what dogs and foxes look like caught in the lamp, but these were like nothing I'd seen before.'

The animal set off at speed and Rogers reported his sighting to Mrs Rhodes. Later they found tracks of a large catlike animal with 4-inch paw prints and made a cast of them. When Mrs Rhodes contacted the Ministry of Agriculture, an official dismissed the killings as the work of dogs.

Mrs Rhodes was angry. 'They just won't listen,' she said. 'You'd think they would have learnt from their mistakes in Devon. It's like a giant cover-up. They don't know what to do about the animals, so they just pretend they don't exist.'

It is not difficult to understand her frustration. I stood on a hill on West Dartmoor and could see from my vantage point both the hills of South Molton and the area of Nine Stones in Cornwall. The sites are linked by heavily-wooded valleys and forested moorlands which would provide ample cover for a roaming cat to cross between the two. Yet, in spite of their acceptance that possibly more than one wild panther-type cat was living in the area around South Molton, the agricultural authorities were dismissing the possibility of a cat just a few miles away in the next county ignoring the evidence of the slaughtered sheep and eye-witness reports.

Here was the same sort of prejudice that had hampered the start of Operation Beastie on Exmoor in 1983. Nine years of experience seemed to have been wasted on the Ministry of Agriculture. Or could their apparent lack of concern stem from a more sinister motive?

Throughout my years investigating the existence of the mystery big cats of Britain I have constantly come up against the suggestions of a cover-up. At first, I used to dismiss the idea, putting it down to no more than the frustrated anger of farmers, but over the years I have discovered incidents that, when put together, provide a worrying aspect to the attitude of the authorities.

The first incident to cause disquiet involved the photographs of Tonmawr cats taken by Steve Joyce in South Wales in 1982. He proudly announced to the press that he had taken the photographs, stating that he had sent them for processing. The photographs had all been shot on the same night, and those of both the adult cat and the two smaller cubs, were interspersed with other test shots taken between the appearances of the animals. For some months sightings had been reported in the area of two houses at the foot of a hill, the animals eventually being lured by bait into a garden where they were observed by the local residents over a period of weeks, and finally photographed.

When I arrived, Steve Joyce had just received the film back from processing with every shot supposedly showing the cat and cubs as blank. It could have been put down to a dud film or a fault in the camera had not all the intervening test shots come out perfectly.

Everyone involved was convinced that the film had been tampered with, perhaps to destroy proof that they had been seeing anything other than domestic cats. What made them so suspicious was the success of the intervening test shots. If the camera or the film had been faulty in any way or if the photographer were incompetent, then the test shots should not have succeeded either. At the same time, I did not believe in outside interference, any more than I considered that the spoiling was due to supernatural causes. A more reasonable explanation was the excitement of the photographer when the animals were present. Perhaps this caused him to make a simple mistake, such as forgetting to remove the lens hood.

The camera still contained an unfinished film, which included some shots taken on the same night. We arranged for someone to come and process the remaining film in Anne Magg's kitchen, and the results were two photographs of the cub-like animal, showing very clearly its grey coat with dark thin stripes and spots. This second film proved that the witnesses had indeed seen the animals they claimed to have seen. So why did the shots sent away to be developed – taken by the same man with the same camera, in the same conditions on the same night – fail?

I still could not believe that the first film had been tampered with and dismissed the whole thing as a coincidence. Others were less willing to forget the matter. Many people have voiced to me their suspicions that evidence was being suppressed in order to keep an alarming situation under control. Perhaps the government was afraid, people suggested, that confirmation of big cats roaming at will around the British Isles would cause widespread panic among the population.

It would be an understandable reaction, yet in the areas where I worked I found that the opposite was the case. At

first the idea of panther-size cats hunting in the neighbour-
hood caused fear among residents but, as they came to terms
with the existence of such animals, the fear turned to a feeling
of admiration for the power and intelligence of the creatures.
Where the cats were not preying on farm stock, people often
expressed a sense of pride that they had the creatures living in
their area. Few witnesses wanted to see them dead, or even
caged.

Personally, I never encountered interference with my own
researches from any authority, but I certainly came up against
prejudice, especially in scholarly scientific circles. In print
and on the air, so-called experts constantly rubbished my
work and accused me of either ignorance or lying. But as the
years passed and the sightings increased in number, so
attitudes began to change. The police and Ministry of
Agriculture officials gradually came to accept the seriousness
of the situation and the need for further investigation.

In the summer of 1989 a South Molton man, Brian Crook,
was walking with his wife on the moors when all at once they
became aware of a large panther-size black cat. They stopped
to watch the beast, which remained sunning itself, apparently
unconcerned by their presence. The couple noticed there
were a number of rabbits crouched motionless in the area.
Suddenly the cat rose and walked across to a rabbit that
appeared to be frozen in terror. The cat picked up the rabbit,
the unfortunate creature making no bid to escape, killed it
with a neck bite and calmly proceeded to eat it before moving
away. Mr and Mrs Crook estimate that the sighting lasted
about fifteen minutes.

What amazed them was not the cat but the behaviour of the
rabbits. It was as if they were programmed to remain
motionless until the cat had finished feeding. So fascinated
were Mr and Mrs Crook with what they had seen, they
contacted Trevor Beer, whom they knew to be interested in
big cats, and agreed to take both Trevor and his wife to the
site. When they returned to the area a few days later, Brian

Crook armed with a movie camera, and Trevor Beer, carrying a stills camera, were thrilled to spot the big black cat once more. This time the witnesses were able to film the animal for about five minutes before it bounded off. Very excited, Brian Crook handed his film over to be developed. They all believed that at last they had proof of the existence of the beast. Unfortunately the film was returned from processing blank. This caused more rumours of a cover-up to circulate. It was a repeat of the disappointment of the Tonmawr pictures, and, like the Welsh photographs, the mystery was increased by the fact there were some photographs to back up the witnesses's claims. The movie film was blank but the film in Trevor Beer's stills camera revealed a large black cat. The weather had been perfect, the light good, and they were not rushed with the filming as the creature remained for a few minutes, obviously unconcerned by their arrival.

Steve Joyce had announced publicly he had taken the photographs of the Welsh cats and then sent them off for processing. My own photographs were certainly not tampered with, but I had never made any statement about having taken them before they were actually published. It seems fanciful, yet of the five films I know to have been taken, supposedly showing the mysterious big cats, the only ones to be developed successfully were those that did not receive advance publicity.*

Although a cover-up would seem unlikely, there is perhaps an outside chance that someone in authority, worried about public reaction to a situation that appeared to be getting out of control, could have taken panic measures. Yet surely it would be safer to dismiss such photographic evidence than to destroy it. Photographs cannot be used as proof of the existence of the subject because it is so easy to forge a picture

---

* The lack of documentary evidence and the law of libel prevent me from saying all that I know about this affair.

by using trick photography. A tame big cat, superimposed shots making a domestic cat appear leopard-size, a taxidermist's specimen, a model or even a cardboard cut-out photographed in moorland vegetation – all could produce fairly convincing pictures of Exmoor beasts. Tampering with the unclear, hazy amateur photographs taken by witnesses would not appear to be worth the risk of exposure.

Even a single unidentified skull cannot prove the existence of a species. It could be a mutation or a hybrid, and if photographs and the Dartmoor big cat skull are not proof, is there any clear evidence to support a large mystery feline species prowling across the British countryside undetected by the scientists? Of the panther-size predator, no, not yet. Though any minute of any day, the ultimate proof may finally be found – either an animal shot, killed accidentally, or the carcase of an animal that has died of natural causes.

All the same, there is definite evidence that scientists who are opposed to the possibility of the British big cat do not always know just what is in fact living wild in the British Isles.

In 1984 Lord Doune, the son of the Earl of Moray, wrote to me about a gamekeeper in the north-east of Scotland who had found the body of a dog-size black cat in a snare. Although the animal was not large enough to be an adult big cat, it could have been a cub. The carcase had been lost but photographs taken of the body were used to publicise a search for other similar cats in the area. Farmers and gamekeepers responded immediately with claims that they had been shooting large black cats on Highland estates for years. The first specimen I saw was a taxidermist's preservation of a cat from the Kellas Estate in Morayshire. At once it was obvious that whatever the mystery Scottish black cat was, it had no relationship with the sheep-killing panther-size feline that had been reported in the same area. The Kellas cat, a fully developed adult male, was the size of a Scottish wildcat (*Felis silvestris silvestris*), larger than a domestic cat but nowhere near the size of a leopard.

The Scottish wildcat is a native British species, unlike the domestic cat which is believed to have bred from the African wildcat (*Felis silvestris lybica*) and arrived long ago with settlers, probably the Romans. Larger than the domestic cat, the Scottish wildcat is tabby, the broad head displaying a distinctive M pattern. It has small wide-set ears, a striped fawn or grey coat, and a bushy, ringed, blunt-ended fairly short tail. Although not a big cat, it has a reputation for ferocity and an instinctive aggression towards humans, but its size prevents it being a danger to prey larger than a hare or a very young lamb. The species can be found across Europe, but melanism has never in the past been recorded in the wildcat population.

The immediate scientific response to the black Kellas 'wildcat' was to call it a hybrid between a domestic cat carrying the black gene and a Scottish wildcat. Even this theory caused a small amount of argument as some scientists refused to accept that hybridisation could occur between the two species and dismissed the Kellas as a very large feral domestic cat.

Although many scientists were convinced that the Kellas cat was of no further interest, I felt it was well worth investigating the claims that large black 'wildcats' were frequently killed on the north-east Scottish estates. The claims were true, and eventually I obtained a number of identical black wildcats from over a wide area of the Scottish Highlands. I moved to Morayshire to live and collected the carcases of the Kellas cats while still continuing my investigations into the existence of the British big cat.

The media understandably confused the two species – the panther-size, sheep-killing cat, of which we lacked a specimen, and the smaller fierce Kellas cat – and this in turn confused the public. Photographs of the Kellas cats were published with the suggestion that they were connected with the sheep-killings. Claims were even made that the Kellas cats were the result of hybridisation between escaped pumas and domestic black cats. Ridiculous as this theory is, some people believed it. One scientist announced that the Kellas felines were evolving cheetah-like adaptations, despite the lack of any evidence to back his theory.

For eight years I tried to persuade the scientific establishment to investigate the origin of the Kellas cats and presented my specimens to the Natural History Museum in London, the Zoology Department of the University of London, the International Society of Cryptozoology, and other individuals in the academic world of science. Finally Dr Andrew Kitchener of the Royal Museum of Scotland agreed to carry out a taxonomic study of the animals.

Most of the Kellas specimens that I obtained were dead. Then, in 1986, the television programme 'Tomorrow's World' produced a live Kellas-type female cat that had been trapped on the Kellas Estate. Two years later a superb male specimen was captured in Inverness-shire. These two cats were kept until 1991 in the Highland Wildlife Park at Kincraig, where they failed to breed successfully. The pair was then gifted to me. Despite their ferocity and secretive nature, I was able to form a relationship with the cats, although they could never be tamed. When they became secure and learnt to trust me, they finally succeeded in producing the first Kellas kittens ever recorded as seen by man. Some scientists had predicted what the kittens would look like, if any arrived. In the event, they were mistaken.*

Although the Kellas cats have no direct relationship with the larger sheep-killing mystery felines of Britain, they proved that scientists could be wrong to ignore reports of sightings of other strange animals at large in the countryside. If a felid the size of a small dog can exist for years undetected by zoologists in the Scottish Highlands, then clearly not all our wildlife is safely categorised and identified. But could it

* The full story of the Kellas cats is told in a book, *My Highland Kellas Cats*, to be published by Cape in 1993, together with the results of Dr Kitchener's study of the animals.

really happen twice? Could there be not one but two mystery feline species living wild in the British Isles – the Kellas cat and a leopard-size feline?

It would appear there could be, not two, but three.

In 1988 a gamekeeper from the Dufftown area in Speyside, north-east Scotland, killed a large black cat that he believed to be of the Kellas type. The body was deep-frozen for me to collect, no one suspecting, that it was anything other than another Kellas specimen. When I saw it I knew at once that the Dufftown cat was not a true Kellas. It was the size of a Kellas cat, with a slender body, long legs, a sleek black short coat and a long whip-like tail. The head of the creature was the most striking feature. The animal looked like a hybrid between a cat and a rabbit. The ears were large, almost hairless and set upright, the forehead sloped from a flattened skull, the nose had a pronounced bump and wide nostrils, and the upper jaw overshot the lower. The cheekbones were high and broad, giving the eyes an almost oriental slant. The canine teeth were very long, the lower teeth fitting into grooves in the upper jaw, the upper canines protruding below the lower jaw.

While the outer appearance of the Dufftown cat was curious enough, the identity of the animal became even more baffling when the body was skinned and the skull cleaned. The overall shape and texture of the skull was strange, the bone itself of a fiberous creamy composition. The top of the cranium was noticeably indented, the skull long and narrow with a broad nasal passage and protruding upper jaw. The lower jaw bones were heavy, broad and straight. Although the skull itself was as big as that of a fairly large wildcat, the cranial capacity was very small, giving the animal a brain about half the size. A domestic cat has a larger brain than the Dufftown cat in a smaller skull.

If the skull shape was different to that of either the wildcat or the domestic cat, the dentition was positively freakish. The upper jaw had only two premolars instead of four, and the incisors were pointed and interlocking, giving the animal a saw-like bite. The powerful jaw with its vicious teeth, the big ears with correspondingly large ear drums, the pronounced nose and the small brain, all suggested a perfect killing machine, hunting by scent and sound, but with limited intelligence.

What has been the scientific response to the Dufftown cat? It has been dismissed. One suggestion was that it might be a hybrid of a wildcat and a Siamese cat. Anyone who could propose that idea cannot be familiar with the Siamese breed, which has a delicate pointed face, in contrast to the heavy jaws and protruding features of the Dufftown animal.

The Dufftown cat is an adult male and, at the time of writing, the only specimen discovered. Perhaps we will find others and eventually study the creature's genetic make-up and trace its origin. Until then, the skinned body and internal organs remain preserved, waiting for the scientific world to become interested in its existence.

The two smaller cats do not prove the existence of the mystery British big cat but they do establish the fact that the countryside of this crowded island can be populated with animals unsuspected by zoologists past and present. The huge Dartmoor skull, with its terrifying canines, may be the first physical proof of the third and most exciting of the mystery British felines. Dr Andrew Kitchener has undertaken to re-examine the skull and look seriously at the evidence for the existence of the big cat.

Something is out there preying on farm stock and providing tantalising glimpses of a felid prowling across the countryside. It is ten years since the Royal Marines tramped across Exmoor, hunting the beast. The marines have now gone, but the beast or its relatives remain, stalking the grazing sheep and ripping apart the unprotected prey. It is surely time for the scientists to leave the laboratory and join the countryman in the forests and fields of Britain. Whatever is out there can be found. It is doubtful if the killing can be stopped, but it might be possible to control it, once the identity of the killer is known.

And that surely is in everyone's interest, even that of the beast itself.

In January 1993 the renowned Belgian zoologist, Dr Bernard Heuvelmans, wrote: 'The wave of cat-type kills across the whole of the British Isles is alarming. But felids are unobtainable in an incredible way (all over the world)!' Incredible yes, but then truth is often stranger than fiction.

Beast of Exmoor attacks car

A WILDCAT that has been reported stalking Exmoor has hurled itself at a car containing two adults and five children.

The two families today reported the night-time attack by the creature. "We were terrified. It was really big and black with massive teeth and as tall as the side windows of the

by John Passmore

car," said 35-year-old Susan Stretch, who was with her three children, her neighbour Lynn Wardell and her son and daughter, on a quiet lane near Bridgwater, Somerset, when the animal charged at their Citroen. It is the third time in a week the animal had been seen in the area.

The sightings match descriptions from the moor dating back to 1983, of an animal which savaged sheep but escaped attempts by Royal Marines and armed police to shoot it.

Mrs Stretch braked hard when she saw the animal in her headlights near the village of Cossington. She expected it to run away, but it turned and charged straight at the car.

"The children screamed 'Mummy, mummy; it's going to kill us', but there was such a thump as it threw itself against the side of the car that I thought I had killed it," she said.

Postscript

No one should be tempted to think of the big cat mystery as an inexplicable nine-year wonder that has had its day and subsided into folklore. The graphic account reproduced on the page opposite, of an attack by a large black cat on a car in countryside bordering Exmoor, appeared in the London *Evening Standard* on 16th December 1992 – the day before the printer delivered proofs of this book to my publisher. It is not a report that can easily be brushed aside. Here is no vague description of a distant sighting that could be a case of mistaken identity. Such was the impact when the creature charged into the side of the car that one is led to wonder how long it will be before a big cat is so badly injured in a traffic accident it cannot get up and slink away, and we have our first dead specimen.

Looking back through my newspaper cuttings, I have found a significant number of reported near misses in the Somerset/Devon area. Thirty-year-old Andrew Gilpin was riding his motor-cycle home at about midnight in March 1983 when he almost hit a large black cat on the A38 near Chudleigh Knighton. He told the Torquay *Herald Express* 'the animal jumped out about a foot away from me. I was so close I had to lift my leg to avoid hitting it.' He described the creature as about two feet high and three feet long, and it moved fast across the road to the clay pits. In November that year lorry-driver Ray Chilcott was reported in the *North Devon Journal-Herald* as seeing a big black cat between South Molton and Brayford in the early hours of the morning. He said the creature 'went up the road in front of me for about 50 yards. He had short ears that were standing up and a much bigger tail than a dog, half the length of his body.' Two years later, also in November, John Richbell, a Brixham baker, crashed his car while trying to avoid 'a very large catlike animal' that suddenly loped across the main road between Halwell and Dartmouth in front of him.

Encounters with highway pedestrians are also not unknown. In May 1988 ex-soldier Alex Rankine fled in terror after a big cat sprang out of some bushes at him. The former Scots Guard told the Glasgow *Daily Record*, 'It hurtled past me and stood in the road, snarling and spitting at me. There's not a lot that scares me, but this time I was terrified. It was a mottled brown and white colour and the size of a Labrador dog. And it had some set of teeth. The beast took off in one direction and I ran home the opposite way.' A spokesman for St Andrews police said, 'There have been a few reported sightings of some kind of big cat between here and Cupar.'

On 30th October 1992, the *Banffshire Herald* (my local paper in Scotland) carried the headline: 'Sheep Savaged by Wild "Puma". Evidence grows of local wild cat terror.' The *Herald* went on to say 'considerable damage' had now been done to livestock by large wild cats seen roaming the local hillsides, but that local farmers were 'reluctant to talk about the problem.'

The item was of interest but certainly not news. For years there have been reports of black, brown and even grey big cats in the Grange-Cullen area. In 1990 a farmer lost thirty sheep in three months from one field backing on to forest.

With helpers I set up a powerful telescope to observe the site and within days a large black panther-size cat was seen to stalk the ewes, quartering and herding them like a sheep dog, at midday in clear sunny weather. The farmer, unaware of the cat's presence, arrived to check his sheep and the cat immediately took cover behind a heap of stones, emerging to retreat back into the forest when the farmer had left.

Other farms around the site still regularly lose stock to the feline predator. In the spring of 1992 farmers formed nightly patrols along the fringe of the Aultmore forest in an attempt to protect their flocks. The hunters spotted a large black cat on a number of occasions, but failed to shoot it. Two of the farmers got rid of their sheep because of the losses, others moved their flocks away.

Later that summer, farmers from a few miles away in the Mulben area of Speyside approached me to report sightings of a large black panther-like cat. Highland cattle had been stampeded through fencing and a ewe was found with its throat torn out. A night watchman on patrol at nearby distillery buildings suddenly came face to face with a black leopard-size cat. In September 1992 the Scottish folk group Innesfree told me that they had spotted a panther-like dark cat while driving home through the area after a performance. Three months later, the lady delivering the newspapers to my local village shop in Drummuir reported seeing a large brown cat crossing the Dufftown to Keith road. In the same week a man going into the village from the Drummuir Castle estate heard a large animal following him. He said it was a big cat and was too frightened to walk that way home.

Despite all this, the scientists still say that there is not enough evidence to warrant a serious investigation. My sentiments are like those of Dr Gerald Legg, whose letter I quoted at the beginning of this book. He felt that 'this case merits further examination.' I would just add, 'and soon.'

Di Francis
January 1993

Select Bibliography

Bord, Janet and Colin, *Alien Animals*, Granada, 1980

Brown, Theo, *Tales of a Dartmoor Village*, Toucan Press, 1973

Clair, Colin, *Unnatural History*, Abelard-Schuman, 1967

Cobbett, William, *Rural Rides*, 1830

Conan Doyle, Arthur, *The Hound of the Baskervilles*, John Murray, 1917

Francis, Di, *Cat Country*, David & Charles, 1983

Heuvelmans, Dr Bernard, *On the Track of Unknown animals*, Paladin, 1970

Jones, Reverend Edmund of Tranch, *Newport: A Relation of Apparitions of Spirits in the County of Monmouth and the Principality of Wales*, 1813

Ricciuti, Edward R., *The Wild Cats*, Windward, 1979

Rudkin, Ethel H., *The Black Dog*, Folklore, 1938

Tate, John, *Genette, Where is She Now?*, Lion Publishing, 1985